Gospel Light's

SONFORCE KIDS

SPECIAL AGENTS

Reproducible!

Assemblies & Skits
Production Guide

with Bible Story Skits, Puppet Production Tips and Closing Program

HOW TO MAKE CLEAN COPIES FROM THIS BOOK

You may make copies of portions of this book with a clean conscience if

>> you (or someone in your organization) are the original purchaser;

>> you are using the copies you make for a noncommercial purpose (such as teaching or promoting your ministry) within your church or organization;

>> you follow the instructions provided in this book.

However, it is ILLEGAL for you to make copies if

>> you are using the material to promote, advertise or sell a product or service other than for ministry fund-raising;

>> you are using the material in or on a product for sale; or

>> you or your organization are not the original purchaser of this book.

By following these guidelines you help us keep our products affordable.

Thank you,

Gospel Light

Gospel Light Vacation Bible School

Senior Managing Editor, Sheryl Haystead >> **Senior Editor,** Heather Kempton Wahl >> **Editor,** Karen McGraw >> **Story Consultant,** Matthew Luhn >> **Editorial Team,** Mary Davis, Becky Garcia >> **Contributing Editors,** Diana Beckett, Cindy Lunden, Sherri Martin, Judy Nyren

Art Directors, Lori Hamilton, Samantha A. Hsu, Lenndy McCullough >> **Senior Designer,** Carolyn Thomas

Founder, Dr. Henrietta Mears >> **Publisher,** William T. Greig >> **Senior Consulting Publisher,** Dr. Elmer L. Towns >> **Senior Consulting Editor,** Wesley Haystead, M.S.Ed. >> **Senior Editor, Biblical and Theological Issues,** Bayard Taylor, M.Div.

CONTENTS

CUSTOMIZE YOUR VBS!

Choose from these options:

>> *Assembly Skits*
>> *Stunts*
>> *Bible Story Previews*
>> *Puppet Production Tips*

MAKE THIS YEAR'S ASSEMBLY SKITS COME ALIVE BY USING MULTIMEDIA! SEE PAGES 5-6.

Why Use This Guide?

This guide provides everything needed to have fun, exciting assemblies that your students will love! The purpose of the skits, stunts and leader conversation suggested for the assemblies is to introduce the key topic and Bible truth that will be emphasized throughout the rest of that session.

In addition to the stunts, Bible story preview improvisations and skits suggested as performance options during the assemblies, there is a Promotional Skit and a Closing Program. Use the Promotional Skit to advertise your VBS in your church and/or community. Present the Closing Program at the end of VBS for families to attend and enjoy what their kids did during VBS.

We have also included Bible story skits that can be used to supplement the stories told in the Bible Story Center. They are particularly useful for older students who may already know the Bible stories. Instead of passively listening to a story, they can be active participants by acting out the stories for their peers or for classes of younger students.

Finally, this guide provides production information and tips for using puppets in your assemblies and classrooms.

New This Year!

Every church makes VBS its own. We want to provide you with the options you need to customize the assemblies to suit your church, staff and students. Of course, keep your daily schedule and the time frame for assemblies in mind as you choose your options! For more information about the individual options, see "Opening Assemblies" on this page.

Evangelism and Skits

Because the skit characters in all but the Bible story skits are fictional, we do not show them experiencing spiritual conversion, nor do these characters present the plan of salvation. Gospel presentations by fictional characters can blur the line between the truth of the gospel and funny, occasionally slapstick fiction. We feel the gospel plan of salvation is best presented by a real person who the children know and with whom they have a relationship—rather than by an actor playing a fictional character. Therefore, conversation about becoming members of God's family is provided in the Conclusion of each day's Bible story (see any age-level *Bible Story Center Guide*).

Opening and Closing Assemblies

For additional ways to add fun and excitement to your assemblies, see "Assembly Suggestions" in "Bonus Theme Ideas" in your *Director's Guide*.

Each day at SonForce Kids, staff and students alike will enjoy gathering together for some large-group fun and Bible learning.

You may choose to have preschool children attend the assemblies or have various skit characters visit the individual early childhood classrooms to lead children in a review of the memory verse and the session's focus.

Opening Assemblies

An assembly, led by the VBS Director or a volunteer, begins each session in Mission Command at SonForce Agency's satellite station. Pennants, to be displayed at the front of the Assembly Hall, present each session's Daily Mission. Use Daily Mission Pennants (available from Gospel Light) or reproduce the patterns found in *Reproducible Resources* onto poster board.

Gathering

Here are some tips for getting your students into the assembly room and seated:

>> Have classes sit with teachers and helpers.

>> Seat younger children in the front of the assembly room.

>> Have a helper for each team hold a group sign or post signs in areas where groups gather and sit. Not only will the signs identify the groups for activities during the assemblies, but they will also help latecomers know where to find their classes.

>> If you are gathering in a large area without chairs or pews, you can put down blankets or large lengths of fabric in different colors for groups to sit on. This can sometimes help contain kids who might otherwise wander.

Assembly Options

The basic components of the assemblies (Bible Memory Verse, Prayer, Song, Review, etc.) all contribute to an understanding of the focus for each session. In addition, we encourage you to customize your opening assembly to suit your staff, students and time frame. For each session, we include three fun performance options: an exciting stunt, a fun improvisation and a traditional skit. For each session, read the suggested options and use as many or as few as you want, and arrange them in whatever order best suits your VBS!

Stunts

These stunts are performed by kids and staff and help kids discover the key word from each Daily Mission. Choose these stunts if you love a lot of audience participation—and you don't mind making a bit of a mess!

Bible Story Preview

For those churches with outgoing individuals who think quickly on their feet and love to perform for kids, we've included a set of improvisations about each day's Bible story. You can use these improvisations during the Opening Assembly to preview the Bible story students will hear later in the session or during the Closing Assembly as a review of the Bible story.

These improvisations feature special agents who wear black suits and sunglasses and think they are very hip and cool. However, they don't always know exactly what they're doing as special agents. Kids learn with these agents as they try out different spy skills and discuss the session's Bible story.

Three Basic Rules of Improvisation:

1. **Always say "yes" to your partner.** Agree with and build on what your partner says. Disagreeing or saying "no" stops the action.

2. Unless your partner is already expecting it, **don't ask questions**. Questions can put your partner on the spot and stop the action.

3. **Stay in the present.** Talking about the past or future is just talk and can get boring quickly. Talk in the here and now to promote action that is always more interesting than just talking.

Assembly Skits

The Assembly Skits are designed to catch the students' attention and introduce the session's lesson focus. They are traditional skits with well-rehearsed lines and stage directions. Be sure to read the other sections of this guide devoted to preparing the assembly skits.

The skits take place at the fictional SonForce Agency, a satellite station orbiting high above its home planet Earth. The agency was created to allow kids the opportunity to perform special missions for which they are uniquely qualified. Miss Newton is the head of the agency and is responsible for training SonForce special agents like Inez Halley, Edward Clark Felton and the newest agent, Jack Oort. Jack brings with him a robot he built named . . . Robot.

Children will laugh and at times find themselves on the edge of their seats watching the characters deal with the threat of an Earth-bound asteroid. The dialogue provided for the assembly leader at the end of each skit will help your students make the connection between the skit and the session focus.

Multimedia

Because of this year's high-tech theme, the assembly-skit scripts include use of video and slides to make the skits a multimedia experience. We recommend using a large screen and projecting the images onto it. However, you may choose to use a television monitor and DVD player.

If your church has someone experienced

in video editing, make the most of the resources available to you to add graphics, text, special effects, etc. to the videos you create.

 **SonForce Logo Animation** (Used at the beginning of each skit, as well as the Promotional Skit and Closing Program.) This animation is provided on the *The Asteroid Incident Skit DVD*.

Slides (Used in Skit 1.) These still photographs are used to introduce your team of SonForce agents. See the Session 1 Skit Script for photograph directions. Prepare slides to be shown during the skit, or use a slideshow program to display the photographs.

Space Federation Ambassador (Used in Skits 2 and 4.) This is a video character with whom other actors interact. Using the same actor who plays Miss Newton, film this character's lines ahead of time and then show the video at the time indicated in the script. Be sure your actor pauses between each line to allow time for the live actors to say their lines when the skit is presented. The actor should continue to act during these pauses, giving appropriate facial expressions and reactions even when not speaking.

Confession Video Used in Skit 5. This is a portion of the story action in Skit 2 that is dramatically revealed to the other characters during Skit 5. Videotape the highlighted portion of Skit 2, shooting from Robot's perspective, with only Felton on the screen. If available, use a fish-eye lens for comic effect.

Note: Our sketches show the projection screen at center stage. Your church may have screens on one or more sides of the stage. A side screen will work fine. If you have two screens, use one or the other but not both. The Ambassador will have to look to the side as if looking at the characters. This will work for one side screen, but on the other side screen, it will appear as if he or she is talking to the wall!

Closing Assemblies

Helpful Hint: Check out the bulletin boards at www.gospellightvbs.com. These discussion groups give you the opportunity to exchange skit production tips with directors from all over the United States and Canada. Discover proven methods to set the stage and to get your actors up and running.

At the Closing Assembly, students will review the memory verse and again have the session focus reinforced before being dismissed with a tantalizing glimpse of what's going to happen during the next session.

Star Prize

During each Closing Assembly, award a Star Prize to the class judged to be the best in a serious or silly category. Classes may win the prize for having the most students on time, singing the loudest, bringing the most visitors, sporting funny hairstyles, bringing their Bibles, wearing the same color, memorizing the most verses, wearing space-exploration or special-agent clothing, raising the most money for a missions or service project (see "Missions Center Guide" in *Director's Guide*), etc.

The prize need not be elaborate or expensive. However, it should be something the class can carry as it travels to centers and assemblies. Here are some suggested prizes: a Daily Mission Pennant or posterboard reproduction (see "Opening and Closing Assemblies," p. 4) attached to a long stick, a large inflatable or stuffed star or rocket ship, several bead or crystal stars and one or more model planets attached to a long stick with fishing line, a moon- or star-shaped Mylar balloon.

Note: Make sure that each class is recognized at least once during the week. Award prizes to more than one class during each Closing Assembly if necessary.

Assembly Skit Casting

Choose five people to play the parts of Miss Newton/Space Federation Ambassador, Inez, Felton, Jack and Robot. The script calls for two female and three male actors; however, feel free to adapt any or all of the characters to accommodate the gender of your actors. Choose people who have a sense of humor and some dramatic ability. They need to commit to attending rehearsals in order to be fully prepared for each skit.

Make Your Characters Come Alive

The key to making your skit characters come alive is to have each one develop a clearly defined personality. The students will get to know the characters and enjoy anticipating how each one might react in different situations. Development of a character includes the following:

>> **Movements**—Each actor should practice movements that reflect his or her character's personality, such as a way of walking, a stance, a gesture of the hands or a strong, emphatic way of entering and leaving the stage. For example, Miss Newton often pats her oversized wig.

Actors should always remember to face the audience when they speak and never to cross in front of another actor when he or she is speaking.

>> **Speech**—Each actor should speak in a voice that accentuates his or her character's personality. Each actor should also take note of phrases that are important or typical of his or her character and practice saying them in ways that will be memorable to the children without sacrificing clarity. For example, Robot normally speaks without much emotion, but it is only while under Felton's control that he speaks mechanically.

>> **Costumes**—Although the characters all wear the same basic costume, black pants and a black SonForce Kids T-shirt, you can still enhance the individual characters with accessories (see pp. 8-9). If you don't have all of the suggested items, substitutions can easily be made. Thrift stores, yard sales and the closets of congregation members are good sources of inexpensive (or free) costumes.

>> **Continuity**—Actors should remain in character whenever around VBS students. Kids love interacting with the skit characters! If possible, it's great for skit characters to participate in games, activities and Closing Assemblies with students.

Rehearsal

Rehearsal is essential to the success of your assembly skits. Actors must be totally familiar with characterizations, spoken lines and positions onstage. Confident, well-prepared actors will present the message of the skit clearly and powerfully. Rehearsal also allows actors the opportunity to be creative and flexible. They can add their own expressions, gestures or movements to customize their characters.

Rehearsal will also help actors get used to performing with the video character, the Space Federation Ambassador. The timing of their lines will depend in great measure on the pauses in the video.

Have someone watch each rehearsal and comment if actors are positioning themselves correctly on the stage; speaking slowly, loudly and clearly; using appropriate expressions and gestures, etc.

The Asteroid Incident Skit DVD can help you prepare for your live performances. A fully staged production of the five session skits on this DVD provides ideas for the backdrop, props and costumes. The DVD can also help your volunteer actors develop facial expressions, vocal inflections and gestures. (You may even choose to show the DVD instead of performing live skits.)

Assembly Skit Characters

Leader—The Assembly Leader leads large-group assemblies (Opening Assembly, Closing Assembly, Closing Program, etc.). This job is often performed by the VBS Director, Youth Leader or Skit Leader. The leader is enthusiastic, charismatic and able to capture and keep the interest of kids in large-group settings. The Assembly Leader dresses in clothing consistent with the theme of SonForce Kids (see suggestions under "Bonus Ideas" in the *Director's Guide*).

Miss Newton/Space Federation Ambassador— These two characters are played by the same person. Miss Newton is the Head of the SonForce Agency. She is authoritative and a bit fussy, but has the best interest of each agent at heart. She wears a very elaborate wig—a fact disclosed to everyone in the first skit, to her complete and utter humiliation. The Space Federation Ambassador appears only as a video character with whom the other actors interact. Neither character seems to notice their resemblance to each other.

Inez Halley—A 12- to 14-year-old girl who has been a SonForce agent for several years. Very bright and intelligent, she looks for logical explanations for everything. Underneath, her compassion for others shines through. Her greatest aspiration is to become a "Starmada" pilot and she will work as hard as she needs to in order to become one.

Jack Oort—A 12- to 14-year-old boy is a new agent at the SonForce Agency. A technological and com-

Space Federation Ambassador

Video monitor

Miss Newton

Glasses

Elaborate wig

Suit

Inez Halley

Badges for Levels 1 through 4

Bracelets

Note: All SonForce agents wear black pants and a black T-shirt with the SonForce logo.

puter genius, he has been teamed up with Inez so that she can orient him to the agency. Jack tends to be very enthusiastic, and he doesn't always think before taking action.

Edward Clark Felton—A 12- to 14-year-old boy, Edward has been at the agency for several years. He is very intelligent and technologically savvy, but not very nice. Overly polite and accommodating to authority figures, he is mean and conniving with other agents. He especially dislikes Inez and Jack, who have talents and abilities that threaten his high-ranking position at the agency.

Robot—Jack's cybernetic invention, Robot wants nothing more than to be as human as possible. His speech and movements are dispassionate, but still relaxed and somewhat human. It is after Felton takes control that Robot's behavior and speech become decidedly mechanical and stiff—robotic.

SonForce Agency Special Agents Each day you may wish to reward a few VBS students by inviting them to be "extras" on the set. Dress them in black pants and black SonForce Kids T-shirts, and have them walk on and off the stage or gather together when a meeting is taking place.

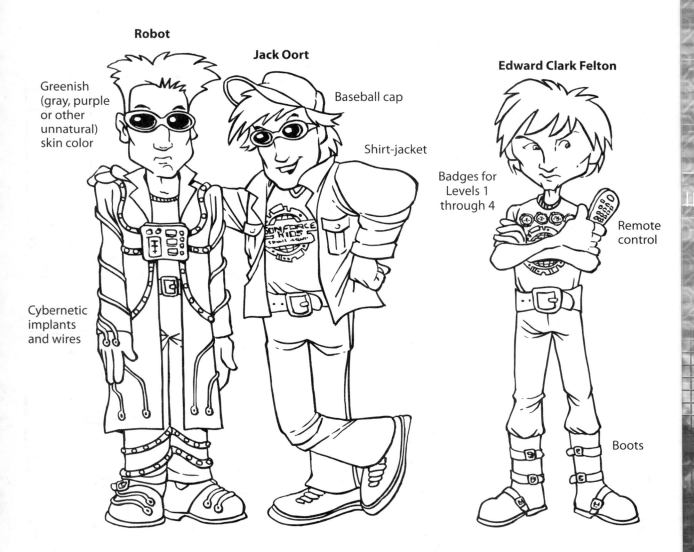

Robot

Jack Oort

Edward Clark Felton

Greenish (gray, purple or other unnatural) skin color

Baseball cap

Shirt-jacket

Badges for Levels 1 through 4

Remote control

Cybernetic implants and wires

Boots

Note: Use Agent Light Hand for one or both of Robot's hands (available from Gospel Light).

Mission Command Backdrop and Constructed Props

A large painted scene of Mission Command will add color and provide an interesting backdrop for the skits. Talk with someone in your church or community who is familiar with painting backdrops, and determine which material would work best for your backdrop (paper, fabric, cardboard, muslin and wood react differently to various kinds of paints). Make your backdrop at least 8x10 feet (2.4x3 m), preferably the same width as your stage.

Photocopy the Mission Command Backdrop Pattern (see p. 12) onto a transparency. Use a transparency projector to enlarge the design onto your backdrop material and trace the design with pen or pencil. Paint background colors first, adding details after the background has dried.

Optional: To really give your backdrop a hi-tech look, poke or drill holes in the backdrop and from the back, insert different colors of Christmas lights to make the control panels sparkle. Poke or drill holes in the starry sky and insert white twinkle lights to make the stars twinkle. Cut holes where the monitors would be and behind the backdrop mount working monitors on tables to show through the openings. Tape the openings to the sides of the monitor for a secure fit. On the monitors, display slideshows of stars, planets and other astronomical objects.

Center Console—Measure the top of a rectangular table. Copy the measurements onto a piece of thin plywood. Extend the length of one side and then draw a curve along opposite side to create half an oval (sketch a). Cut out, paint and place on table. Measure the curved edge and cut butcher paper to fit (make sure butcher paper is large enough to go from top of table to floor). On butcher paper, glue or tape lengths of holographic paper to make two borders. In between borders, cut seven equally spaced circles. Cover holes with different colors of acetate. Tape butcher paper to front of table (sketch b). Place Christmas lights behind each acetate circle. (Note: If you have to run electrical cords across stage, tape cords down to stage so that actors will not trip over them.)

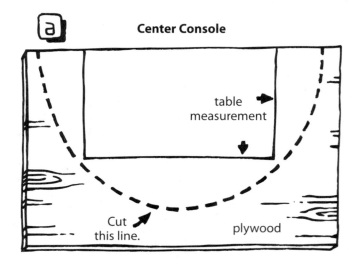

a | **Center Console**

table measurement

Cut this line.

plywood

b

Bathroom Set—Enlarge Bathroom Backdrop Pattern (p. 13) onto a large sheet of cardboard or plywood so that it is 6 to 8 feet (1.8 to 2.4 m) wide and about 6 feet (1.8 m) tall. Paint and cut out. Paint the floor of the bathroom to match the stage floor or the linoleum, if you are using a sheet of linoleum under the cutout and commode. Nail wood to each end and the center of both sides of the cutout to make triangular supports so that the cutout stands securely (sketch c).

Construct a door frame the same height as the finished cutout and attach at the point where the last stall door would be (sketch d). Use hinges to attach a plywood door. Attach a thin strip of wood to side of door frame opposite hinges to act as a stop. Paint door frame and door to match other stalls on Bathroom Set. Attach a roller latch so that actors can secure door shut from either side of door (sketch e). Attach handle to outside of door.

Bathroom Set

Mission Command Backdrop Pattern

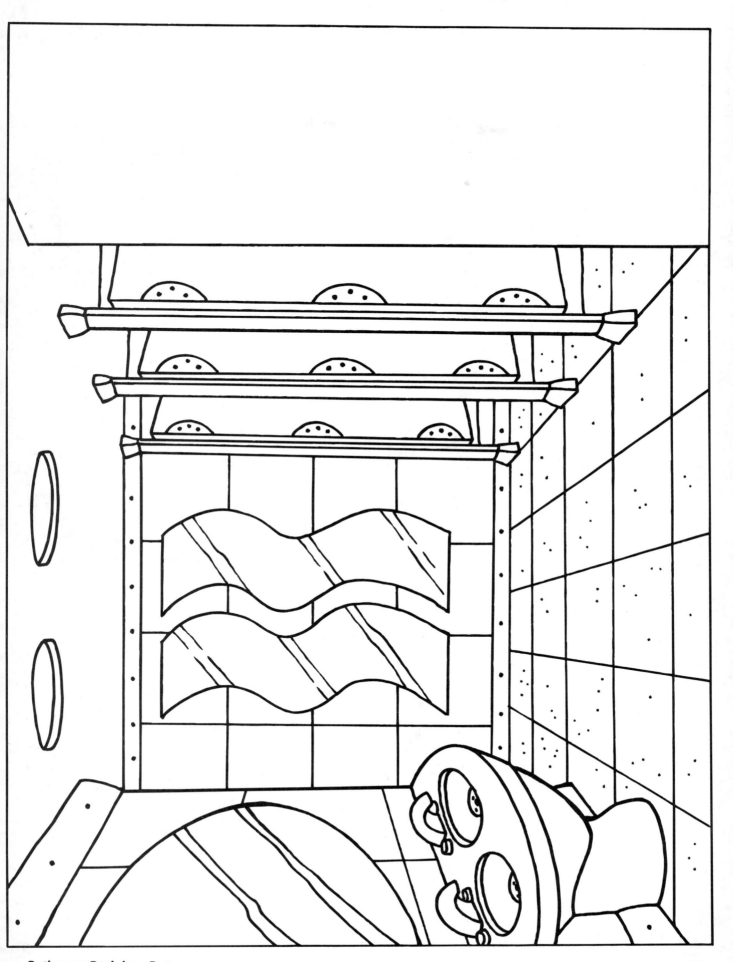

Bathroom Backdrop Pattern

Badge Patterns

SonForce Kids Logo Pattern

Assembly Skit Setup

The Mission Command Backdrop is used with various other elements to suggest the location of the skits: Mission Command at the SonForce Agency's satellite station. (See pp. 10-11 for instructions on constructing the necessary props.)

Use the list of props on page 20 to ensure you have all the items necessary to dress the set and prepare your actors for each skit.

Session 1

Place Center Console at downstage center. On top, place a computer setup (monitor, keyboard, mouse, etc.) at each end. Lower large projection screen, or set one up if needed.

Make sure Slides 1, 2 and 3 are loaded into the slide projector or that the slideshow program is prepared and ready to be projected onto large screen.

Hand remote control to Felton.

Session 2

Place Center Console at downstage center. On top, place a computer setup at each end. Lower large projection screen, or set one up if needed. Place Bathroom Set at the far right of the stage. Set up commode behind the stall with the working door.

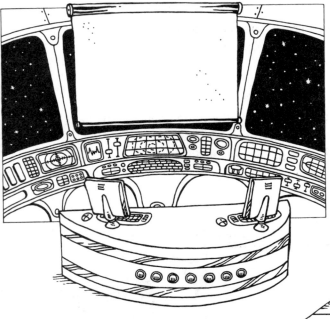

Place cleaning supplies and toilet brushes in buckets. Place filled buckets behind Center Console.

Hand screwdriver to Felton to place in a pocket.

Session 3

Place Center Console at downstage center. On top, place a computer setup at each end.

Place the bonding strip off stage right.

Session 4

Place Center Console at downstage center. On top, place a computer setup at each end. Lower large projection screen, or set one up if needed. Place Bathroom Set at the far right of the stage. Set up commode behind the stall with the working door.

Use bonding strip to tie Inez and Jack together as at the end of the Session 3 skit. Leave end of strip free for Robot to use as a lead.

Session 5

Place Center Console at downstage center. On top, place a computer setup at each end. Lower large projection screen, or set one up if needed.

Place cleaning supplies and toilet brush in bucket. Place filled bucket behind Center Console.

Hand remote control to Felton.

Props

For each skit, you will need the Mission Command Backdrop (see p. 11) and the appropriate costume for each character (see pp. 8-9). Each individual skit also calls for the following props (mainly household items). All props should be gathered well ahead of time. Publish a list of needed items in your church bulletin. If some items can't be located, modify the skit to use something else.

> **Prop Master:** You may wish to assign one or two people to take charge of gathering props, placing them on stage before each skit and returning them to the owners or to storage following VBS.

Promotional Skit

__ *SonForce Kids CD* and player

__ *The Asteroid Incident Skit DVD*, player and monitor or large screen

__ "SonForce Logo Animation" from *The Asteroid Incident Skit DVD*

__ yellow light

Session 1

Opening Assembly

__ Bible with marker at Jeremiah 17:7

__ *SonForce Kids Songbook, CD* and player

__ word chart for song "God's Kids"

__ "Trust" Daily Mission Pennant or poster-board reproduction (see "Opening and Closing Assemblies," p. 4)

Stunt

__ whiteboard

__ dry-erase markers

__ 4 rolls of toilet paper

Bible Story Preview

__ newspaper

__ scissors

__ chair

Assembly Skit

__ *SonForce Kids CD* and player

__ Center Console (see p. 15)

__ 2 computer setups (monitors, keyboards, mice, etc.)

__ Slides 1, 2 and 3 (see descriptions in Skit Script)

__ slide projector and large screen

__ remote control

__ red light

Closing Assembly

__ Bible with marker at Jeremiah 17:7

__ *SonForce Kids Songbook, CD* and player

__ word chart for song "I Trust You with My Life"

__ "Trust" Daily Mission Pennant or poster-board reproduction (see "Opening and Closing Assemblies," p. 4)

__ Star Prize(s) (see p. 6)

Session 2

Opening Assembly

__ Bible with marker at Romans 12:10

__ *SonForce Kids Songbook, CD* and player

__ word charts for songs "God's Kids" and "Be Strong and Courageous"

__ "Unite" Daily Mission Pennant or poster-board reproduction (see "Opening and Closing Assemblies," p. 4)

Stunt

__ whiteboard

__ dry-erase markers

__ cosmetic grease pencil

__ canned shaving cream

__ 2 or more bedsheets

__ 2 to 5 chairs

__ plastic spoons

__ towels

Bible Story Preview

__ 2 briefcases

__ cheese or peanut butter

__ crackers

Assembly Skit

__ *The Asteroid Incident Skit DVD*, player and monitor or large screen

__ Center Console (see p. 15)

__ Bathroom Set (see p. 11)

__ 2 computer setups (monitors, keyboards, mice, etc.)

__ commode

__ 2 buckets

__ cleaning supplies, including 2 toilet brushes

__ screwdriver

Closing Assembly

__ Bible with marker at Romans 12:10

__ *SonForce Kids Songbook, CD* and player

__ word chart for song "Together in Harmony"

__ "Unite" Daily Mission Pennant or poster-board reproduction (see "Opening and Closing Assemblies," p. 4)

__ Star Prize(s) (see p. 6)

Session 3

Opening Assembly

__ Bible with marker at Proverbs 19:20

__ *SonForce Kids Songbook*, CD and player

__ word charts for songs "God's Kids" and "Be Strong and Courageous"

__ "Train" Daily Mission Pennant or poster-board reproduction (see "Opening and Closing Assemblies," p. 4)

Stunt

__ whiteboard

__ dry-erase markers

__ package of large flour tortillas

__ scrap paper

__ marker

__ large bowl

Bible Story Preview

__ Optional: strobe light

Assembly Skit

__ *SonForce Kids CD* and player

__ Center Console (see p. 15)

__ 2 computer setups (monitors, keyboards, mice, etc.)

__ bonding strip (neon-colored marking tape, holographic ribbon, etc.)

__ red light

Closing Assembly

__ Bible with marker at Proverbs 19:20

__ *SonForce Kids Songbook*, CD and player

__ word chart for song "Train Me Up"

__ "Train" Daily Mission Pennant or poster-board reproduction (see "Opening and Closing Assemblies," p. 4)

__ Star Prize(s) (see p. 6)

Session 4

Opening Assembly

__ Bible with marker at Jeremiah 7:23

__ *SonForce Kids Songbook*, CD and player

__ word charts for songs "God's Kids" and "Be Strong and Courageous"

__ "Follow" Daily Mission Pennant or poster-board reproduction (see "Opening and Closing Assemblies," p. 4)

Stunt

__ whiteboard

__ dry-erase markers

__ scrap paper

__ marker

__ large bowl

Bible Story Preview

__ none

Assembly Skit

__ *SonForce Kids CD* and player

__ *The Asteroid Incident Skit DVD*, player and monitor or large screen

__ Center Console (see p. 15)

__ 2 computer setups (monitors, keyboards, mice, etc.)

__ bonding strip (neon-colored marking tape, holographic ribbon, etc.)

__ red light

Closing Assembly

__ Bible with marker at Jeremiah 7:23

__ *SonForce Kids Songbook*, CD and player

__ word chart for song "Obey Me!"

__ "Follow" Daily Mission Pennant or poster-board reproduction (see "Opening and Closing Assemblies," p. 4)

__ Star Prize(s) (see p. 6)

Session 5

Opening Assembly

__ Bible with marker at Joshua 1:9

__ *SonForce Kids Songbook*, CD and player

__ word charts for songs "God's Kids" and "Be Strong and Courageous"

__ "Lead" Daily Mission Pennant or poster-board reproduction (see "Opening and Closing Assemblies," p. 4)

Stunt

__ whiteboard

__ markers

__ 5 tin pie plates

__ 25 plastic insects

__ whipped cream

__ plastic tablecloth or bedsheet

__ towels

Bible Story Preview

__ none

Assembly Skit

__ *SonForce Kids CD* and player

__ *The Asteroid Incident Skit DVD*, player and monitor or large screen

__ Center Console (see p. 15)

__ Bathroom Set (see p. 11)

__ 2 computer setups (monitors, keyboards, mice, etc.)

__ commode

__ bucket

__ cleaning supplies, including toilet brush

__ remote control

__ red light

Closing Assembly

__ Bible with marker at Joshua 1:9

__ *SonForce Kids Songbook*, CD and player

__ word chart for song "Mission of Love"

__ "Lead" Daily Mission Pennant or poster-board reproduction (see "Opening and Closing Assemblies," p. 4)

__ Star Prize(s) (see p. 6)

Closing Program

__ *SonForce Kids CD* and player

__ *The Asteroid Incident Skit DVD*, player and monitor or large screen

__ Daily Mission Pennants or poster-board reproductions (see "Opening and Closing Assemblies," p. 4)

Bible Story Skits

Session 1

__ large basket

__ unfinished basket

__ reeds for weaving

Session 2

__ large platter

__ variety of toy food

__ table

__ table decorations (candles in candlesticks, floral centerpiece, dishes, glasses, silverware, etc.)

__ long sheet of paper

__ thin stick 12 to 16 inches (30.5 to 40.5 cm) long

Session 3

__ None

Session 4

__ table

__ two chairs

__ scroll (long sheet of paper rolled up from both ends)

__ thin stick 12 to 16 inches (30.5 to 40.5 cm) long

__ rocks and sticks

__ red, orange and yellow tissue paper

__ plastic or other blunt knife

Session 5

__ None

Assembly Prop Checklist

The following checklist is a master checklist for props used in the Opening and Closing Assemblies ONLY. They are listed in order of use. For specifics on the items, see detailed Prop lists on pages 18-19.

Cross off items for those performance options (Stunt, Bible Story Preview, Assembly Skit) you choose not to do.

PROPERTY (see detailed prop lists on pp. 18-19)	SOURCE (VBS supplies, Sunday School supplies, church member, etc.)	Date RECEIVED	Date RETURNED
OPENING AND CLOSING ASSEMBLIES			
Bible			
SonForce Kids Songbook			
SonForce Kids CD			
CD player			
word charts for songs			
Daily Mission Pennants			
or poster-board reproductions			
Star Prize(s)			
STUNTS			
whiteboard			
dry-erase markers			
4 rolls of toilet paper			
cosmetic grease pencil			
canned shaving cream			
2 or more bedsheets			
2 to 5 chairs			
plastic spoons			
towels			
package of large flour tortillas			
scrap paper			
markers			
large bowl			
5 tin pie plates			
25 plastic insects			
whipped cream			
plastic tablecloth or bedsheet			
BIBLE STORY PREVIEWS			
newspaper			
scissors			
chair			
2 briefcases			
cheese in a squeeze-top can			
crackers			
strobe light (optional)			
ASSEMBLY SKITS			
SonForce Kids CD			
The Asteroid Incident Skit DVD			
CD player			
DVD player			
Monitor or large screen			
Center Console			
2 computer setups			
Slides 1, 2 and 3			
remote control			
Bathroom Set			
commode			
2 buckets			
cleaning supplies			
screwdriver			
red light			
bonding strip (neon-colored marking tape, holographic ribbon, etc.)			

Promotional Skit

Materials: See prop list on page 18.

Preparation: Make sure *The Asteroid Incident Skit DVD* is ready to be projected onto large screen and "SonForce Logo Animation" are cued up to play.

Skit Script

(*Play "SonForce Logo Animation" from* The Asteroid Incident Skit DVD. Inez, Jack *and* Robot *enter from stage left and cross to center.*)

Inez: (*Raising hand in greeting.*) **Hello! I'm Inez Halley and this is Jack Oort. We're from SonForce Agency's satellite station high above Earth. We are special agents with a mission!**

Jack: (*Also raising hand.*) **Hi!** (*Pointing to* Robot *with thumb.*) **This is Robot.**

Robot: (*Tapping* Jack *on shoulder.*) **Jack? I AM a robot. But I don't like being called Robot. It's not a real name.**

Jack: Can we talk about this later? We're here to tell everyone about SonForce Kids VBS!

Robot: What's a "VBS"?

Inez: (*Explaining.*) **"VBS" stands for Vacation Bible School. And all these people** (*Indicates audience.*) **from (name of church) are going to have SonForce Kids Vacation Bible School!**

Robot: (Felton *enters from stage left.*) **But what's a Vacation Bible School? There is no information in my database.**

Felton: Vacation Bible School is a (weeklong) program of fun and adventure!

Inez and Jack: Hello, Felton.

Inez: (*To audience.*) **This is Edward Clark Felton, another SonForce agent.**

Felton: You mean the TOP agent, don't you? (Jack *rolls his eyes as* Inez *shakes her head.* Felton *turns to* Robot *and looks him up and down.*) **I hope your robot is prepared for your demonstration. Wouldn't it be embarrassing if something went wrong?** (*Laughs.*)

Jack: We're ready. (*To audience.*) **The demonstration will be the first day of VBS, (date VBS starts). So be sure you're here!**

(*An offstage voice is heard, "Edward Clark Felton: Please report to Miss Newton's office for special assignment."*)

Felton: (*With conceit.*) **Hear that? Miss Newton is giving ME a special assignment. Not you** (*Points to* Inez.) **or YOU** (*Points to* Jack.). **That's because she realizes who the BEST SonForce special agent is. ME!** (*Laughing, he exits stage right.*)

Inez: Maybe during SonForce Kids VBS he'll figure out what being a special agent is REALLY about.

Robot: Will VBS teach about being special agents?

Jack: You bet! And not just ordinary special agents. It's all about having courage and being special agents for God!

Inez: And it's all done with loads of great activities like fun-filled games . . .

Jack: Delicious snacks . . .

Inez: Creative crafts . . .

Jack: Exciting skits . . .

Inez: And fascinating TRUE STORIES from the Bible.

Robot: That sounds great!

Jack: (*To audience.*) **You're gonna LOVE VBS—and VBS is bound to help all of you become better special agents.**

Inez: So get ready for an out-of-this-world adventure. SonForce Kids special agents—courageous kids on a mission for God!

(Inez *and* Jack *give information about VBS times and dates, where and when registration will begin and/or how to sign up to be a VBS volunteer. All exit.*)

Session One

TRUST
In God's Plans

Opening Assembly/Skit

Note: Customize your assemblies! These opening assemblies include a number of components: Welcome, Song, Stunt, Bible Story Preview, Skit Script, Bible Memory Verse, Prayer, Song, Announcements and Dismissal as well as three performance options (see p. 5). Use those components that most appeal to you or for which you have time. Do not feel you have to include ALL the components in your assembly time.

Materials: See prop list on page 18.

Preparation: To prepare for the **Stunt**, set whiteboard at center of stage. Place dry-erase markers and rolls of toilet paper beside whiteboard. Draw five blank lines on the whiteboard, one for each letter of the key word from the Daily Mission, "TRUST."

To prepare for the **Bible Story Preview**, cut peep holes in a section of newspaper. Place a chair at center stage. Give cut newspaper to one of the actors.

To prepare for the **Assembly Skit**, set stage and prepare actors as directed in "Skit Setup" (see p. 15). Cue Slides 1, 2 and 3 to be projected onto large screen. Cue "SonForce Kids Theme" to play from *SonForce Kids CD.*

Play songs from CD as children gather. Give "Trust" Daily Mission Pennant or reproduction to a volunteer to hold up during assembly.

Welcome

Leader: Welcome to Mission Command at the SonForce Agency. We're going to have a great time training to be special agents for God! If you're excited to be here like I am, stand up with me. When I call your group name, wave your hands high and shout "SonForce" as loud as you can! (Leader *enthusiastically guides each group to respond in turn.*)

Song

Leader: Let's get started with a song about being SonForce Kids! (Leader *leads singing of "God's Kids."*)

Stunt

Stunt Performers: Select one adult volunteer (VBS director, activity leader, church pastor, etc.) and four VBS students.

Stunt Action: This is an action-packed version of Hangman. Hand a roll of toilet paper to each of the four student volunteers. Call on individual students in the audience to guess a letter of the alphabet.

If the letter guessed is not in the word "trust," write the letter on the edge of the whiteboard. If the letter guessed is in the word, write the letter on the correct blank line(s). Students may guess the word only after at least three letters have been filled in on the board.

Every time that a correct letter is guessed, all four student volunteers run to the adult volunteer who stands still with arms at his or her sides. Students wrap toilet paper around the arms and torso of the adult volunteer for five seconds. To enforce the five-second rule, lead the audience to count aloud together: "One-thousand-one, one-thousand-two, one-thousand-three, one-thousand-four, one-thousand-five!" On the audience count of five, the adult volunteer tries to lift his or her arms to try to get free. You may wish to select a new group of student volunteers after each group has a turn to wrap.

At the end of the improvisation, the Leader comes forward and speaks to the audience. **Today we're going to talk a lot about TRUST and how trusting God's plans can help you have courage to be the best SonForce Kids agent you can be!**

Bible Story Preview

Improvisation Performers:
Two adults dressed in black suits, with white shirts, black ties and dark sunglasses.

Improvisation: Instead of using names, actors refer to each other by their initials. One enters and sits at center stage, opening a newspaper which has several peepholes cut in it. After pretending to read the newspaper for a short time, he or she begins to look through peepholes, surveying the audience while staying hidden behind the paper. The second agent enters and sees the first, walks up to him or her, watches for a few moments from several angles, pantomiming questioning motions, and then taps the agent on the shoulder and asks what he or she is doing. The first agent jumps, the newspaper flies, and the first agent describes what he or she was doing—keeping watch on the audience and trying to remain hidden. He or she then mentions that this is just like what someone in the day's Bible story had to do. Both agents encourage the audience to pay attention later during the Bible story and find out why a young girl named Miriam was keeping watch.

Skit Script

Leader: This week at SonForce Kids you'll get to meet some special agents from SonForce Agency's satellite station. So let the adventure begin! (Leader *exits stage left. Lights are lowered.* "SonForce Kids Theme" *plays as* Miss Newton *enters and crosses to center stage.*)

Miss Newton: (*Gesturing broadly.*) Welcome to SonForce Agency! I am Miss Newton, the head of the satellite training station, orbiting high above our home planet, Earth. The SonForce Agency was created to allow kids the opportunity to perform special missions for which they alone are uniquely qualified. The only admission requirement is to be willing to serve! Of course, to make the most of the experience, we recommend agents make the best possible use of the unique talents and abilities God has given them. Here are a few of the agents you will get to know. (*She gestures to a large screen on which slides are projected.*)

(*Slide 1: Show a still shot of* Inez *smiling and posing with hands on hips.*)

Miss Newton: Inez Halley has been a SonForce agent for six years. She is a Level 4 agent. The highest rank is Level 5. Level 5 agents get the most important, exciting missions. Inez hopes to become a pilot in the Intergalactic Starmada.

(*Slide 2: Show a still shot of* Felton *with a sneering, haughty expression, posing with arms crossed on his chest.*)

Miss Newton: Edward Clark Felton has also been a SonForce agent for six years and is a Level 4 agent. He and Inez are currently our highest-ranking agents.

(*Slide 3: Show a still shot of* Jack *smiling and posing with his arm around* Robot.)

Miss Newton: Finally, meet one of our newest agents, Jack Oort. Jack brings great computer and technological skill to SonForce Agency. He has teamed up with Inez on a special project. In a few moments, we will see a demonstration by a robot Jack created and Inez helped to program. If they succeed, Inez will advance to Level 5 and Jack will be the first agent in SonForce HISTORY to begin at Level 5! Now make yourselves at home while I see to a few details before the demonstration. (*Walks off stage left.* Jack, Robot *and* Inez *enter from stage right.*)

Inez: (*Seriously.*) Okay, Jack. Are you sure you programmed Robot with the proper coordinates?

Jack: For the thousandth time, YES! Robot is ready. (Felton *enters from the audience, unobserved by the others. He remains hidden, eavesdropping on the others.*)

Robot: I don't mean to complain, Jack, but I wish I had a real name. "Robot" just seems so . . . mechanical. (*Sighs.*) I'd feel much more human with a name.

Jack: Tell you what, Robot, you can choose a name for yourself—after the demonstration is a success!

Inez: (*Walks around* Robot *examining him.*) I'd feel a lot better if we'd run another simulation this morning. You never know what might have happened to him overnight.

Jack: (*Confidently.*) What could happen? A meteor shower mess up his electrical circuits? No way!

Robot: Don't worry, Inez. I feel confident we will succeed.

Felton: (*Stepping forward, mocking them. Sarcastically.*) Feel? Imagine that . . . a robot that wants a name and who "feels." (Felton *laughs.*)

Inez: Knock it off, Felton! Jack's programmed Robot to respond with appropriate emotional expressions for any number of situations.

Robot: (*Dispassionately.*) This is true. I am able to accurately measure the emotional responses of humans around me. (*To* Felton.) For instance, you are currently experiencing irritation.

Felton: (*Sneering.*) As if a robot knows anything about emotions . . .

Robot: Disgust.

Felton: (*Angrily.*) You interrupted me!

Robot: Anger. Outrage.

Felton: (*Shaking his fist at* Robot.) Stop it, you lousy bucket of bolts! (Miss Newton *enters from stage right.* Felton *immediately stops shaking his fist and begins patting* Robot *on the shoulder.*) What a fine robot you are! (*He turns to* Miss Felton *and smiles ingratiatingly.*) Why, hello, Miss Newton. I was just giving my best wishes to Inez and Jack for today's demonstration.

Miss Newton: Well, that's certainly nice of you, Edward. I'm sure you too will one day work your way up to Level 5.

Felton: (*Meaningfully.*) Oh, yes . . . Some day VERY soon!

Miss Newton: (*Slightly confused by his answer, she shakes it off and turns to* Inez *and* Jack.) Okay, I hope you two are ready. As you can see, everyone (*She indicates audience.*) is assembled and ready to see your demonstration. Just what will your robot do?

Jack: (*Proudly.*) In record time, Robot will map a navigational chart between any two places in the galaxy, taking into account current atmospheric anomalies like an ice storm on Saturn or tornadoes on Jupiter! (Jack *turns to the audience.*) Starting from SonForce Agency, where do you want to go? (Jack *encourages responses from audience. Choosing one, he continues.*) (Pluto)! Robot, what is the best route?

Felton: (*To audience.*) Okay, you guys, watch this! (*Unobserved by* Miss Newton, Inez *and* Jack, Felton *holds out a remote control. He points it at* Robot *and presses a button.*)

(*Play "Haywire" sound effects from CD.* Robot *begins moving erratically, jerking his head, arms and legs.* Robot *stumbles over to* Miss Newton, *grabs her wig and pulls it off. She screams and covers her head with one hand while trying to snatch the wig back from him as he jerks around.* Inez *and* Jack *try to stop* Robot, *ad-libbing "Oh, no!" "Robot, stop!" etc.* Felton *laughs uproariously.*)

Robot: (*Still jerking around, keeping wig away from* Miss Newton *and speaking erratically, voice rising and falling in tone, volume, speed, etc.*) Observable emotions: humiliation, irritation, anger, panic . . . Looks like you're having a bad hair day! (*As sound effects diminish,* Robot *winds down and finally collapses on the floor.* Miss Newton *grabs her wig and shoves it back on her head sideways.*)

Miss Newton: (*Flustered and upset.*) **Inez! Jack!! Get that robot out of my sight! I don't ever want to see that . . . that . . . metal monstrosity again!** (Inez *and* Jack *help* Robot *to its feet.*) **Oh, I'm so disappointed in you two! I thought I could trust you!**

Inez: (*Protesting.*) **You CAN trust us!**

Jack: **We don't know what went wrong!**

Miss Newton: (*Struggles to straighten out her wig—and her dignity.*) **I'm afraid there's no way you can move up to Level 5 now.** (Felton *grins wildly and shakes his fists over his head in victory.* Miss Newton *glances his way and he immediately drops his hands and feigns a concerned look.*) **In fact, Inez, you've been demoted to Level 1.** (*She removes all but the Level 1 badge from* Inez's *uniform.*) **And Jack, you'll begin at Level 1. You both obviously need a LOT more training before you're ready for any important missions.** (*Suddenly, red lights flash on and off three or four times. Play "Red Alert" sound effect. Flustered.*) **Red alert! We've got a red alert!** (*Speaking to audience as well as characters on stage.*) **Stay here! I'll be right back.** (*She runs off stage left.*)

Inez: **Jack, what happened with Robot?**

Jack: **I have no idea! Everything should have worked . . . I'll have to give Robot a thorough diagnostic . . .**

Felton: (*Interjecting.*) **Uh, you'd better leave the robotics work to me. Go find yourselves a nice, easy little Level 1 job.** (*Laughs.*)

Inez: **He's right, Jack. Only Level 4 agents are allowed to do robotics programming. We'll have to leave Robot with Felton for now.** (Felton *grabs* Robot *by the arm and pulls him aside.*)

Miss Newton: (*Enters from stage left, distraught.*) **Oh, no! It's a catastrophe! An asteroid is headed straight for SonForce satellite station. The asteroid is so large, it will smash us to tiny bits.** (*All*

except Felton *gasp.*) **The asteroid will then crash into Earth!** (*Lights go out and all exit.*)

Leader: (*Enters from stage right as lights come up.*) **Whoever tries to stop the asteroid will need a LOT of courage. I wonder which of our agents we can trust to help us. This is a very scary situation! It isn't always easy to have courage—especially when things are scary. But special agents who serve God know that He can give them the courage they need.**

Bible Memory Verse

Leader: During each session at SonForce, we'll have a Daily Mission to help us remember what we're learning about courage. What is today's Daily Mission? (*Volunteer holds up "Trust" Daily Mission Pennant or reproduction.* Leader *pauses as audience answers "TRUST in God's Plans."*) **Even in scary situations, we can trust that God knows what's best for us. So even when we're scared, worried or upset, we can have courage and trust in God's plans.** (Leader *opens Bible and reads Jeremiah 17:7.*) **What does this verse tell us about people who trust in the Lord? They are . . .** (Leader *pauses for audience to respond by saying "blessed."*). **God is greater and more powerful than anything! Isn't it great that He loves us and has plans for us? We can trust in Him and know that His plans are the very BEST plans.**

Prayer

Leader: Dear God, thank You for loving us and having plans for us. Please help us learn to trust You more each day. In Jesus' name, amen.

Song

(Leader *leads singing of "God's Kids."*)

Announcements/ Dismissal

(Leader *explains procedure for Session 1 and dismisses students to classes.*)

Closing Assembly

Song

Leader: Let's sing one of the songs we've learned today! (Leader *leads singing of "I Trust You with My Life."*)

Prizes

(Leader *distributes Star Prize(s) [for more information, see p. 6].*)

Review

Leader: I'm glad you were here today at the SonForce Agency, learning about what it takes to be a SonForce special agent! (*Volunteer holds up "Trust" Daily Mission Pennant or reproduction.*) **What was today's Daily Mission?** (Leader *pauses as audience answers "TRUST in God's Plans."*) **In today's Bible story, we learned how Miriam and her mother showed courage and trusted God to protect the baby from Pharaoh. What was the baby's name?** (Leader *pauses as audience answers "Moses."*) **Let's say today's Bible Memory Verse together.** (Leader *guides audience in reciting Jeremiah 17:7 aloud.*)

Prayer

Leader: Dear God, thank You for loving us. Thank You for Your plans for us. Help us to have courage to trust in Your plans. In Jesus' name, amen.

Announcements/ Dismissal

Leader: (Leader *makes announcements and invites children back for the next session. Inez enters and stands next to* Leader.) **Come back (tomorrow)** when we'll hear Inez say:

Inez: Miss Newton, Jack and I will be proud to take on this challenge. I know with the two of us working together, we can find a way to stop that asteroid!

Leader: Come back tomorrow to hear more about how working—or uniting—with others can give us courage. We'll also hear about a queen who united with her people to have courage to help them.

Tip: Select a student, or one student from each age level, to say the verse aloud before all students recite it together. Each session, select a different student or students to say the verse.

UNITE
With God's People

Opening Assembly/Skit

Materials: See prop list on page 18.

Preparation: To prepare for the **Stunt**, set whiteboard at center of stage. Place dry-erase markers beside whiteboard. Draw five blank lines on the whiteboard, one for each letter of the key word from the Daily Mission, "UNITE." Next to whiteboard, spread one or more bedsheets on the floor. Place chair on the bedsheet(s). Place another bedsheet on the chair.

To prepare for the **Bible Story Preview**, place the cheese or peanut butter in one briefcase and the crackers in the other. Hand a briefcase to each actor. If not using Center Console for assembly skit, place a table at center stage.

To prepare for the **Assembly Skit**, set stage and prepare actors as directed in "Skit Setup" (see p. 16). Cue video of Space Federation Ambassador to be projected onto monitor or large screen.

Play songs from CD as children gather. Give "Unite" Daily Mission Pennant or reproduction to a volunteer to hold up during assembly.

Welcome

Leader: Welcome back to SonForce Agency's Mission Command! If you're ready for another day of learning to be special agents for God, raise your hands high, stomp your feet and shout "SonForce!" (Leader *enthusiastically guides everyone to respond*.) **Today we're going to learn even more about having courage and being special agents who serve God.**

Song

Leader: Let's sing our song about being a team of special agents! (Leader *leads singing of "God's Kids."*)

Stunt

Stunt Performers: Select two to five adult volunteers (VBS director, activity leader, church pastor, etc.) and a similar number of VBS students.

Stunt Action: Before game begins, select adult volunteers. Out of view of the audience, have a helper use cosmetic grease pencil to print one or more letters from the word "unite" on each adult volunteer's face. (The number of letters depends on the number of volunteers.) Helper then covers letters with shaving cream.

Assign a student to each adult volunteer. Hand students a spoon. Adults each sit in a chair. Students drape sheets over adults and then use spoons to shave adults' faces. When a student uncovers a letter, he or she calls out the letter. Write the letter on the correct blank line on the whiteboard. Students continue shaving until all the letters are uncovered. Use towels to clean up as needed.

Bible Story Preview

Improvisation Performers: Two adults dressed in black suits, with white shirts, black ties and dark sunglasses.

Improvisation: Instead of using names, actors refer to each other by their initials. Actors begin at opposite ends of stage and come sneaking on together, each walking backwards and carrying a briefcase. Play "SonForce Kids Theme" from *SonForce Kids CD* or other "special-agent" music. Agents look around suspiciously, ducking behind things and turning around quickly to see if they are being followed. They slowly near each other, eventually backing into each other, startling both.

Agents greet each other by doing an elaborate and funny secret handshake and exchanging secret code words. They each open their briefcases. One takes out the cheese or peanut butter, and the other takes out the crackers. They discuss how neither snack would be as good without the other as they prepare the snack on Center Console or table.

Agents continue to talk with each other and audience about how an agent alone is not as good as two or more agents united together. Agents encourage audience to listen to today's Bible Story and hear how a queen and her people united together.

At the end of the improvisation, the Leader comes forward and speaks to the audience. **Today your mission is to find out how you can UNITE with others to be a better special agent for God!**

Skit Script

Leader: Our SonForce special-agent friends are going to need a LOT of courage. They just got news that something is about to crash into the SonForce satellite station and then smash into Earth! What is it? (*Pause for audience to say*

"an asteroid.") **Let's see what happens today!** (Leader *exits stage left.*)

Ambassador: (*On large monitor. Miss Newton, Inez, Jack, Felton and Robot enter and take positions watching the large screen. Robot stands with head down, still suffering the effects of having gone haywire.*) **Hello, Miss Newton and all the SonForce special agents. This is the Space Federation Ambassador. As you have no doubt heard, headed toward SonForce Agency is an asteroid so large it will smash the agency to tiny bits. From there, the asteroid will course on until it crashes into the middle of Saskatchewan, causing a cataclysmic event!**

Miss Newton: We heard! Who is going to take care of the problem? Will the Intergalactic Starmada pilots blast the asteroid to smithereens?

Ambassador: The Starmada is in training on the other side of the Milky Way. There's no time for them to get here. As a matter of fact, the only agency close enough to help is YOU!

All except Robot: (*Incredulously.*) **US?!**

Ambassador: Yes, YOU. Miss Newton, I realize most of your agents are in training and normally we would never impose on them to help. But this time there is no choice. The fate of every SonForce agent and every human on Earth is in the hands of you and your agents. Don't fail us.

All except Robot: We won't!

Ambassador: Good-bye and remember: We're all counting on you to succeed with this mission. (*Monitor goes black.*)

Jack: (*To Inez.*) **Hey, is it just me or does the Ambassador look a lot like someone we know?** (*Points to Miss Newton.*)

Inez: Hush, Jack! (*Turning to Miss Newton.*) **Miss Newton, Jack and I will be proud to take on this challenge. I know with the two of us teamed up together, we can find a way to stop that asteroid!** (*Jack nods enthusiastically as Felton glares.*)

Miss Newton: Well, I saw how seriously you took your last mission—you turned it all into a big joke on me! I'm not about to risk lives for another joke! (*Calling.*) Edward Clark Felton! Come here. (*He steps forward.*) As the highest-ranking agent here at SonForce it's up to you to use your considerable intelligence and talent to solve this problem.

Felton: Yes, Miss Newton. You know you can always count on me!

Robot: (*Briefly lifts his head.*) Arrogance. (*Felton turns to glare at* Robot *as* Robot's *head drops again.*)

Miss Newton: What did he say?

Felton: (*Dropping the glare, he smiles ingratiatingly.*) Oh, nothing, Miss Newton. He's still malfunctioning. I'll take care of it. (*Felton takes* Robot *by the arm and exits stage right.*)

Miss Newton: Thank you, Edward.

Jack: But what about us? Is there something we can do to help?

Miss Newton: (*Turns to look at him.*) Well, yes, there is. (*She pulls out two buckets with toilet brushes from behind center console and hands them to* Inez *and* Jack.) The bathrooms on Deck Seven need a thorough cleaning. (*She exits stage right.*)

Jack: (*Despairingly.*) But cleaning toilets is just . . . gross!

Inez: Jack, I'm not happy about being a Level 1 agent, either; but there's no shame in doing a good job at whatever task you're given to do. At least there are two of us working. We'll get done in half the time! I'll take the girls' bathroom and you take the boys'.

Jack: Okay. I'll do it. But I won't LIKE it. (*Inez exits stage left.* Jack *crosses down to Bathroom Set at stage left. Speaking to himself.*) I just hope no one SEES me cleaning the toilets. I've got a reputation to think about! Even if I'm JUST a Level 1 agent. (*He enters the stall closest to audience and starts cleaning toilet.* Felton *and* Robot *enter from*

stage right. Jack *jumps, nervous.*) Uh-oh! Someone's coming! (*He jumps on the toilet and pulls stall door closed behind him.*)

Felton: (*Enters bathroom with* Robot.) Come on, Robot, get in here. I don't want anyone to overhear me.

Robot: I don't like the name Robot.

Felton: Fine! Based on your earlier performance—which was brilliant, by the way—I think I'll call you "Haywire." (*Laughs.*) Yes, Haywire, my friend, you really helped me out by making Inez and Jack look so bad.

Robot: I did not wish to help you. You controlled me with your remote control.

> **Note:** Videotape the segment of this skit that is <u>underlined</u>. This will make the "Confession Video" shown in the upcoming Session 5 Skit. Shoot from Robot's perspective, with only Felton on the screen. If available, use a fish-eye lens for comic effect.

Felton: Yes, and I'll continue to control you. Now, just a few more adjustments and I'll be able to stop you from talking unless I want you to. (*He takes out a screwdriver and appears to be making adjustments behind* Robot's *back, out of sight of the audience.*)

Robot: <u>I could help you in stopping the asteroid. I am fluent in algorithms and calculating navigational maps and basic programming in force field . . .</u>

Felton: <u>I don't need your help in stopping the asteroid, you piece of junk. I ALREADY control the asteroid.</u> (*Jack reacts in surprise, almost dropping his toilet brush.*)

Robot: <u>You control the asteroid? I don't understand.</u>

Felton: (*Leans in close to* Robot.) **Just like I was able to control you with my remote control. I can do the same thing with the asteroid.**

Robot: **But how will that control the asteroid?**

Felton: **I programmed my remote to control an engine I installed inside an asteroid last summer at the Bluelaser Asteroid Recreation Camp. So I started the asteroid on its course and only I can stop it.**

Robot: **But why do you want to make everyone think the asteroid is going to crash into SonForce Agency and the Earth?**

Felton: **Duh . . . So I can be the HERO! And that will make everyone like me. I'll definitely be made a Level 5 agent. Besides, the asteroid really WILL crash into the agency and the Earth. Unless I stop it!** (*He makes a final adjustment.*) **There! I'm done.** (*He puts screwdriver in his pocket and steps forward.*) **Finally! Your questions were starting to bug me. Now you'll only speak in response to me.**

Robot: (*Mechanically.*) **Yes, Master.**

Felton: (*Laughing.*) **That's more like it.** (*Suddenly looks around as if remembering something.*) **Uh oh . . . Haywire, did you check that the toilet stalls are empty?**

Robot: **Master, the bathroom is secure. Only the last stall door is closed.** (Jack *leans forward from his position standing on the toilet to check the lock on the door.*)

Felton: **Well, then check it! What if someone is hiding in there?**

Robot: **Master, no one uses that toilet. The gravity equalizer doesn't work properly. It's been known to suddenly explode.** (Jack *gags, silently.* Felton *and* Robot *exit stage right and Jack runs from the toilet stall, screaming.*)

Jack: **Aaaack! That's so gross!** (*He shakes himself from head to toe.*) **Ugh.** (*To audience.*) **Did you hear what Felton said about controlling the asteroid? Miss Newton has got to know! But I'm just a Level 1 agent. I don't think she'll believe me. And she's probably still mad about Robot taking off her wig! I can't do this alone . . .** (*Snaps his fingers.*) **I'll find Inez! She'll help me have courage to face Miss Newton!** (*He runs off stage left.*)

Leader: (*Enters from stage left.*) **Did you hear what Jack said right before he ran off stage? Uniting with Inez will give Jack courage to face Miss Newton and tell her about Felton's plan.**

Bible Memory Verse

Leader: **What is our Daily Mission for today?** (*Volunteer holds up "Unite" Daily Mission Pennant or reproduction. Leader pauses as audience answers "UNITE with God's People."*) **God wants us to unite with others who love and trust Him so that together, we can help others.** (Leader *opens Bible and reads Romans 12:10.*) **God wants us to take care of each other, not just worry about ourselves. By standing strong WITH others, we can stand up FOR others! Uniting with others will give us the courage we need.**

Prayer

Leader: **Dear God, please help us have courage to unite with others to stand up for people who need help. In Jesus' name, amen.**

Song

(Leader *leads singing of "Be Strong and Courageous."*)

Announcements/ Dismissal

(Leader *explains procedure for Session 2 and dismisses students to classes.*)

Closing Assembly

Materials: See prop list on page 18.

Play songs from CD as children gather. Give "Unite" Daily Mission Pennant or reproduction to a volunteer to hold up during assembly.

Song

Leader: Let's gather together and sing our song about uniting with others! (Leader *leads singing of "Together in Harmony."*)

Prizes

(Leader *distributes Star Prize(s) [for more information, see p. 6].*)

Review

Leader: We sure have had a lot of fun today at the SonForce Agency! (*Volunteer holds up "Unite" Daily Mission Pennant or reproduction.*) **What was today's Daily Mission?** (Leader *pauses as audience answers "UNITE with God's People."*) **In today's Bible story, who went to the king even though she could have been killed?** (Leader *pauses as audience answers "Esther."*) **Esther united with the Jewish people to fast and pray. Esther needed their help to have courage to tell the king about Haman's plan. Let's say today's Bible Memory Verse together.** (Leader *guides audience in reciting Romans 12:10 aloud.*) **Just like Esther honored her people over herself, we can put others before ourselves.**

Prayer

Leader: Dear God, thank You for giving us others with whom we can unite. Help all of us have the courage we need to stand up for others. In Jesus' name, amen.

Announcements/ Dismissal

Leader: (Leader *makes announcements and invites children back for the next session. Miss Newton enters and stands next to* Leader.) **Come back (tomorrow) when we'll hear Miss Newton say:**

Miss Newton: Genius! That's pure genius, Edward! Oh, I'm so proud of you!

Leader: Hmm . . . I wonder what that is all about. We'll have to wait until tomorrow to find out! Also, tomorrow we'll hear about having courage to make wise choices and about a young man from the Bible who did!

3 TRAIN
For God's Service

Opening Assembly/Skit

Materials: See prop list on page 19.

Preparation: To prepare for the **Stunt**, set whiteboard at center of stage. Place dry-erase markers beside whiteboard. Draw five blank lines on the whiteboard, one for each letter of the key word from the Daily Mission, "TRAIN." Place tortillas near white board. On separate scraps on paper, print each letter of the word "train." Place scraps in large bowl.

To prepare for the **Bible Story Preview**, make sure there is an open area for the actors to move freely.

To prepare for the **Assembly Skit**, set stage and prepare actors as directed in "Skit Setup" (see p. 16). Cue "Red Alert" sound effect to play from *SonForce Kids CD.*

Play songs from CD as children gather. Give "Train" Daily Mission Pennant or reproduction to a volunteer to hold up during assembly.

Welcome

Leader: Hello! If you're ready for more fun here at the SonForce Agency, clap your hands, spin around and shout "SonForce!" (Leader *enthusiastically guides everyone to respond.*) **We've had some great fun learning how to have courage to serve God. Today we're going to discover ways we can train as special agents on missions for God!**

Song

Leader: We've learned several songs here at the SonForce Agency. Let's sing our song about having courage! (Leader *leads singing of "Be Strong and Courageous."*)

Stunt

Stunt Performers: Select up to five adult volunteers (VBS director, activity leader, church pastor, etc.).

Stunt Action: Volunteers take turns selecting a paper scrap from bowl. Hand volunteer a tortilla. He or she bites off pieces of tortilla to form the letter written on the scrap. When done, volunteer holds up tortilla for audience to guess the letter. When the letter is correctly guessed, write it on the whiteboard.

Bible Story Preview

Improvisation Performers: Two adults. One dressed in a black suit, with white shirt, black tie and dark sunglasses. The other is

dressed in a black sweat suit with dark sunglasses.

Improvisation: Instead of using names, actors refer to each other by their initials. The agent wearing the sweat suit is onstage doing various warm-ups, shadow boxing and practicing martial-arts moves. Agent dressed in suit comes onstage and after watching for several seconds with perplexed, puzzled motions, asks what he or she is doing. Agent in sweat suit explains that he or she is in physical training, preparing in case the time comes when his or her "special moves" will be needed. Agent in suit challenges agent in sweat suit and they begin to do a slow-motion, exaggerated and funny fight while "SonForce Kids Theme" from *SonForce Kids CD* or other special-agent music plays. (Optional: Lower lights and turn on a strobe light.) Agent in sweat suit wins fight and talks to other agent and audience about how training really pays off and invites audience to find out how Daniel trained to serve God in the day's Bible story and how Daniel's training made a big difference in his life.

At the end of the improvisation, the Leader comes forward and speaks to the audience. **Training is what we do best here at SonForce Kids! All day you will TRAIN for God's Service—be sure to find out how you can continue training long after VBS is over.**

Skit Script

Leader: Last time, Jack found out that Felton created the problem of the asteroid. Felton wants to fool everyone into thinking he's the only one who can stop the asteroid. He thinks that will make him a hero. But real heroes have courage. And pretending to have courage isn't the same thing. Let's see if Inez and Jack's SonForce training will help them show courage today. (*Leader exits stage right.*)

(*Miss Newton enters from stage right with* Felton. *As they enter, red lights flash on and off three or four times. Play "Red Alert" sound effect. Immediately after, a robotic voice is heard from offstage "Asteroid impact in 2.0 hours." Miss Newton is visibly worried.*)

Miss Newton: Edward, did you hear that? We've only got two hours left! Everything we've tried so far has failed to stop the asteroid! Is there anything you can do?

Felton: Well, Miss Newton, I intend to program our satellite tower with a supersonic "bounce-back" beam. We'll have to wait until the asteroid almost hits us! Then we'll send out the bounce-back beam. The asteroid will bounce off it like a tennis ball hitting a wall! The asteroid will ricochet into a black hole and never bother us again!

Miss Newton: Genius! That's pure genius, Edward! Oh, I'm so proud of you! You've definitely earned Level 5 status. I'm going to contact the Space Federation Ambassador right now so that you'll be given a special commendation. Oh! We'll have a feast! A party! A celebration! And a big cake—

(*Inez and* Jack *enter from stage left, running up to Miss Newton.*)

Inez and Jack: Miss Newton! Miss Newton!

Miss Newton: Oh, Jack! Inez! You'll be so happy to hear the good news: Edward is going to save us from the asteroid!

Inez: But that's what we want to talk to you about.

Jack: Yeah! It's because of Felton that we've got asteroid trouble in the first place! (*Unseen by Miss Newton, Felton gives Jack a dirty look.*)

Miss Newton: What? How can that be?

Inez: Jack discovered that Felton set the whole thing up.

Miss Newton: (*Skeptical.*) Edward made an asteroid attack us?

Jack: Yes! (*Confused.*) Well, no . . . Not exactly . . .

Miss Newton: (*Getting irritated.*) Then what EXACTLY did he do, Jack?

Felton: Yeah, Jack. Explain it.

Jack: (*Getting flustered.* Inez *nudges him*

encouragingly.) Well, I don't know exactly . . .

Miss Newton: (*Sternly.*) You've made a very serious accusation, Jack. You had BETTER know "exactly." Just when did you discover this information?

Jack: (*Lamely.*) When I was cleaning the toilets.

Miss Newton: (*Incredulous.*) You found the information in a toilet?!

Jack: (*Struggling to get his words together.*) No . . . You see . . . I was hiding in the toilet—

Miss Newton: (*Irritated.*) Hiding? You mean goofing off! You were supposed to be CLEANING the toilets!

Felton: (*Thinking quickly.*) I think I know what happened, Miss Newton. Poor Jack here (*Pats* Jack *on the shoulder a bit too hard, but* Miss Newton *doesn't notice.*) must have inhaled too much cleaning fluid and misunderstood me. I stepped into the bathroom to make some quick adjustments on the robot so it wouldn't attack you again—

Miss Newton: (*Pats wig.*) Oh! Thank you, Edward. That's very thoughtful. (Inez *and* Jack *roll their eyes.*)

Felton: While there I mentioned to the robot that I'd learned about asteroids at a recreation park this summer and maybe with his database I could come up with an answer to the problem. (*Falsely modest.*) And well . . . I did!

Miss Newton: (*Beaming proudly.*) You certainly did! Now I'm going to get on with the plans for the celebration to honor you. And you two, (*Points a finger at* Inez *and* Jack.) stay out of trouble and make sure everything is spotless! (*She exits stage right.*)

Inez: Well, Felton, you may have fooled her, but you haven't fooled us. And WE'RE going to stop you.

Felton: (*Confidently.*) I don't see how that will be possible.

Jack: Just wait and see.

Felton: No, I've got a better idea. Why don't YOU wait. (*Calling out.*) Haywire!

Inez: (*To* Jack.) Haywire?!

Robot: (*Entering from stage left, he crosses to* Felton.) Yes, Master.

Inez: (*To* Jack.) Master?! Robot, what happened to you? (Robot *keeps looking at* Felton.)

Felton: He's not going to answer you. He only answers ME. Isn't that right, Haywire?

Robot: Yes, Master.

Inez: (*Sadly.*) Oh, that's so demeaning!

Jack: Yeah. "Haywire" is a crummy name.

Felton: You're just jealous because I have YOUR robot! Haywire, get some bonding strip and tie them up! (*As the dialogue continues,* Robot *exits stage right and retrieves bonding strip. When he enters again, he crosses toward* Inez *and* Jack.)

Inez: What?!

Jack: We're not going to let you tie us up! (Inez *and* Jack *take on fighting poses.*)

Felton: (*Laughs.*) Oh, come on, Jack! You built the robot. You know how strong it is. Don't you realize with one press of its hands you could both be squashed?

Jack: (*Looks at Inez and shrugs dejectedly.*) He's right. Let's give up. (*They both drop the fighting poses and stand straight and still, arms crossed over their chests. During the following dialog Robot proceeds to wrap bonding strip around both of them several times, wrapping around their chests so their legs are free and leaving a length of bonding strip to use as a lead.*)

Felton: That's more like it. Now we'll make sure you two stay out of the way until after I "stop" the asteroid. (*He laughs.*) Once I'm a hero, it won't matter what you say. No one will believe you!

Inez: (*Seething.*) Oh, Felton! You're no hero. You're just a . . . just a . . . BAD GUY! Heroes train hard so that they can have courage to make wise choices that help others—not just themselves! Heroes don't lie and pull stupid stunts that put people in danger—just so they can PRETEND to be heroes!

Felton: (*Yawns.*) Blah, blah, blah, blah, blah . . . Nobody KNOWS that but you. And NOBODY believes you! (*To Robot.*) Now, Haywire, put them inside that broken stall in the boys' bathroom. It's doubtful anyone would find them there, but stand guard to be sure.

Robot: Yes, Master. (*He pulls on the free length of bonding strip to pull Inez and Jack toward stage left. They shuffle along behind him.*)

Inez: (*Eyes wide.*) What? The BOYS' bathroom? (*She opens her hands—still tied to her chest—and covers her eyes.*) I don't want to see this!

Jack: Ack! What if the gravity equalizer explodes?! Oh, gross! (*Gagging, he covers his mouth with his hands which are still tied to his chest. They exit stage left.*)

Felton: (*Calling out.*) Have fun! I'm going to go make myself a hero! (*Laughing, he exits stage right.*)

Leader: (*Enters from stage right.*) Do you think Felton is going to get away with his plan? (*Pause for audience response.*) Inez said Felton wasn't a hero, but a . . . What? (*Pause for audience to respond "Bad guy."*) Felton only seems interested in helping one person. Who is that? (*Pause for audience to respond "Himself."*) Inez said heroes train hard so they can have the courage to make wise choices and help people. As special agents for God, we are in training to have courage to make wise choices.

Bible Memory Verse

Leader: What does today's Daily Mission tell us about how to have courage? (*Volunteer holds up "Train" Daily Mission Pennant or reproduction. Leader pauses as audience answers "TRAIN for God's Service."*) When we train to serve God, we learn what God wants us to do. That helps us have courage, knowing we can make wise choices! (*Leader opens Bible and reads Proverbs 19:20.*) Being wise begins with training to serve God!

Prayer

Leader: Dear God, we love You! We want to know how to serve You better. Help us to have courage and to make wise choices. In Jesus' name, amen.

Song

(*Leader leads singing of "God's Kids."*)

Announcements/ Dismissal

(*Leader explains procedure for Session 3 and dismisses students to classes.*)

Closing Assembly

Materials: See prop list on page 19.

Play songs from CD as children gather. Give "Train" Daily Mission Pennant or reproduction to a volunteer to hold up during assembly.

Song

Leader: Let's sing our song about training to be in God's service! (Leader *leads singing of "Train Me Up."*)

Prizes

(Leader *distributes Star Prize(s) [for more information, see p. 6].*)

Review

Leader: I sure had a lot of fun today with all you SonForce Kids! Did you have fun, too? (Leader *pauses for response. Volunteer holds up "Train" Daily Mission Pennant or reproduction.*) **What was today's Daily Mission?** (Leader *pauses as audience answers "TRAIN for God's Service."*) **In today's Bible story, what did Daniel ask to eat instead of food from the king's table?** (Leader *pauses as audience answers "vegetables."*) **Daniel and his friends wisely chose to please God—and in the end, they were stronger and healthier than the other boys training to serve the king. Let's say today's Bible Memory Verse together.** (Leader *guides audience in reciting Proverbs 19:20 aloud.*) **When we read the Bible and listen to others who know and love God, we will become . . .** (Leader *pauses, inviting audience to respond by saying, "wise."*)

Prayer

Leader: Dear God, thank You for giving us the Bible and people who love You so that from them, we can train to serve You. In Jesus' name, amen.

Announcements/ Dismissal

Leader: (Leader *makes announcements and invites children back for the next session.* Jack *enters and stands next to* Leader.) **Come back (tomorrow) when we'll hear Jack say:**

Jack: (*Smiling confidently, he speaks loudly and clearly.*) **Slortnoc tobor!**

Leader: Um . . . I'm sorry, but WHAT did you just say?

Jack: (*Still confident, he repeats.*) **Slortnoc tobor!**

Leader: Oh. That's what I thought you said . . . Find out what "slortnoc tobor" means tomorrow! We'll learn more about courage and hear about a time a man had to write the same book twice!

Tip: Select a student, or one student from each age level, to say the verse aloud before all students recite it together. Each session, select a different student or students to say the verse.

4 FOLLOW
In God's Path

Opening Assembly/Skit

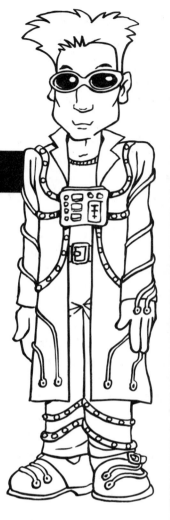

Materials: See prop list on page 19.

Preparation: To prepare for the **Stunt**, set whiteboard at center of stage. Place dry-erase markers beside whiteboard. Draw six blank lines on the whiteboard, one for each letter of the key word from the Daily Mission, "FOLLOW." On separate scraps of paper, print each letter of the word "follow." Place scraps in large bowl.

There is no special preparation for the **Bible Story Preview**.

To prepare for the **Assembly Skit**, set stage and prepare actors as directed in "Skit Setup" (see p. 17). Cue video of Space Federation Ambassador to be projected onto monitor or large screen. Cue "Red Alert" sound effect to play from *SonForce Kids CD.*

Play songs from CD as children gather. Give "Follow" Daily Mission Pennant or reproduction to a volunteer to hold up during assembly.

Welcome

Leader: I'm glad to see all you SonForce Kids. If you're excited to be here, stand up, give a high-five and say "SonForce!" to three people as fast as you can! (Leader *enthusiastically joins in and guides audience to respond. As time permits, repeat activity with children greeting three different people.)* We learn a lot about courage every time we get together here at SonForce Kids. Today we'll discover what it takes to have courage and that it's always best to FOLLOW in God's Path!

Song

Leader: Let's sing our song about being a special team serving God! (Leader *leads singing of "God's Kids.")*

Stunt

Stunt Performers: Select six adult volunteers (VBS director, activity leader, church pastor, etc.) or older VBS students.

Stunt Action: Each volunteer takes a turn to draw a paper from the bowl and act out an object or objects that begin with the letter on the scrap. For example, for the letter *F*, the volunteer might act out "football," "foot" or "frog." Divide the audience into two teams who compete to guess the object and then the letter that begins the name of the object. Write down each letter as it is guessed. (Write *L* and *O* once for each time it is acted out.) Continue until all letters have been acted out.

Bible Story Preview

Improvisation Performers:
Two adults dressed in black suits, with white shirts, black ties and dark sunglasses.

Improvisation: Instead of using names, actors refer to each other by their initials. One of the agents tries to teach the other and the audience the proper procedure for following a suspect. The agents walk around the stage and in and out of the audience. But the second agent just can't get the procedure correct. First he or she follows from too far away and gets distracted; then the agent follows too closely and ends up tripping both agents! Agent doing the training stops to discuss with second agent and audience what it means to follow a leader and how sometimes that doesn't mean following the leader around the room, but following what the leader says to do. Agents challenge audience to listen carefully to the Bible story to hear what it means to follow God and how a man named Jeremiah followed God, even when it was difficult.

At the end of the improvisation, the Leader comes forward and speaks to the audience. **It's important for all SonForce agents to FOLLOW in God's Path. Find out ways you can better follow God today and every day!**

Skit Script

Leader: Yesterday, Jack and Inez showed courage. Even though they were afraid Miss Newton was still mad at them, Jack and Inez told Miss Newton what Felton was up to. Sadly, Miss Newton didn't believe them. Then, Felton had the robot tie up Inez and Jack and hold them as prisoners in the bathroom! Let's see what Inez and Jack do in such a bind. (*Exits stage right.*)

(*Inez,* Jack *and Robot enter from stage left. They are as they were at the end of the previous skit:* Inez *and* Jack *are tied together, shuffling along behind* Robot *who is holding on to the bonding strip. Inez has her eyes covered with her hands. They cross over to Bathroom Set.*)

Jack: Eww . . . I don't want to go into that stall again. It might explode this time! (*Robot puts them in the stall, closes the door and stands in front of the door, arms crossed and not moving.*)

Inez: What are you complaining about? (*She bumps into him.*) Oops! At least you can see where you're going!

Jack: Why are you covering your . . . (*Figures it out.*) Inez, you don't have to cover your eyes! Nobody is in here but you, me and Robot.

Inez: (*Peeks out cautiously before lowering her hands.*) Yes, well, I've never exactly been in a boys' bathroom before. And I hope I'm never in one again!

(*Red lights flash on and off three or four times. Play "Red Alert" sound effect. Immediately after, a robotic voice is heard from offstage: "Asteroid impact in 30 minutes."*)

Jack: Argh! What's important is that we're stuck in a bathroom while Felton is getting away with everything! HE'S going to be made a Level 5 agent, and we're not! We're just Level 1 agents, the toilet cleaners.

Inez: (*With sudden realization.*) Hey, Jack! I just realized . . . It's GOOD that we're Level 1 agents!

Jack: What? Are you crazy? What's good about being a Level 1 agent?

Inez: Well, if you weren't a Level 1 agent, would you have been in this bathroom when Felton told Robot his plan?

Jack: (*Beginning to realize.*) No . . .

Inez: And if you hadn't heard the plan would ANYBODY know about it?

Jack: No! You're right, Inez! If it weren't for my having to clean the toilets, nobody would know what Felton is up to!

Inez: Exactly! It doesn't matter that he's a Level 5 agent—what he's doing is wrong. We may be Level 1 agents, but we're trying to do the right thing. That's what really matters.

Jack: (*Catching her enthusiasm.*) Yeah! (*Then, as quickly as he cheered up, he is suddenly defeated again.*) Yeah. But how can we do the right thing if we can't DO anything? We're tied up in a bathroom!

Inez: True enough . . . Even if we could get free of this bonding strip, Robot is still standing guard. You don't suppose this stall has a BACK DOOR, do you? (*She grins feebly at her joke.*)

Jack: (*Excitedly.*) Back door! That's it, Inez!

Inez: I was just joking! Whoever heard of a toilet stall with a back door?

Jack: Not the bathroom . . . Robot! Programmers often install what we call a "back door" to quickly access our software. I programmed a back door to get into Robot's central processing unit. I'll bet Felton never found it!

Inez: (*Amazed.*) Well, go for it! What do you have to do?

Jack: (*Smiling confidently, he speaks loudly and clearly.*) Slortnoc tobor!

Robot: (*Shakes his head as if clearing it. Then he opens the door.*) Jack! Inez! Are you okay? I'm sorry if I hurt you! (*He leads them out of the stall and starts to untie the bondng strip.*)

Jack: That's okay, Robot. You did great!

Inez: (*Confused.*) What was that you said to get Robot working again?

Jack: (*Explaining.*) Slortnoc tobor.

Inez: (*Still confused.*) Slortnoc tobor?

Jack: Sure! It's "robot controls" backwards! (*He grins.*)

Robot: And it's freed me from Felton's control and allows me to use the artificial intelligence components Jack installed instead of blindly following Felton's commands. Boy, that did NOT feel good! I'm so glad I'll be able to help you now. (*He coils bonding strip and places it back in the toilet stall.*)

Inez: That's great, but time is running short! We've got to get up to the command center and warn everyone . . . (*She suddenly runs out of steam.*) Wait a minute . . . No one believed us before, why would they believe us now? (*She sits down in frustration.*)

Jack: Aha! Well, this time Robot and I have something better than just words to go on.

Robot: Jack?

Inez: (*To Jack.*) What do you mean?

Jack: A "back door" to his controls isn't the only secret I've installed on Robot!

Robot: Jack?

Jack: (*Ignoring Robot.*) Just wait and see! (*He crosses to exit stage left. Inez gets up and tries to catch up to Jack and find out more. Robot follows.*)

Robot: Jack? I thought we were going to do something about my name . . . Jack? (*All exit stage left as Felton and Miss Newton enter stage right. The central monitor lights up and we see the Space Federation Ambassador.*)

Ambassador: Miss Newton? Miss Newton?!

Miss Newton: I'm here, Ms. Ambassador! I want to introduce you to the young man who will save us all! This is Edward Clark Felton.

Felton: Pleased to meet you, Madam Ambassador.

Ambassador: So it's all taken care of? We don't have to worry about the asteroid destroying the Earth?

Felton: That's right, Madam Ambassador. My ingenious bounce-back beam will send

that asteroid into the deepest, darkest black hole. I will save everyone!

Miss Newton: We're so proud of him!

Ambassador: As indeed you should be.

Miss Newton: Ms. Ambassador? This is off the subject, but I've always wondered if we've met somewhere before . . . You seem so . . . familiar . . .

Ambassador: You know, I often thought the same thing about you. But I can't imagine where we might have met before . . .

(*Both pause for a moment, contemplating, and then in unison shrug and say "Oh, well!"* Felton *looks from one to the other and shakes his head in disbelief.*)

Ambassador: At any rate, you obviously run an excellent agency to produce such a fine young man as Edward here.

Felton: Thank you, Madam Ambassador.

Ambassador: Good-bye then! Let me know as soon as the asteroid is bounced away. I expect to hear good news soon! (*The monitor goes out and* Felton *and* Miss Newton *exit stage left.*)

Leader: (*Enters from stage right.*) When Robot was under Felton's control, he did everything Felton told him. But that isn't the kind of obeying God expects us to do—Robot had no choice! Felton controlled everything he did. God made us so that we can CHOOSE to obey Him. As special agents for God, when we choose to obey God and follow in His path, we're choosing the very best path for our lives.

Bible Memory Verse

Leader: What is our Daily Mission for today? (*Volunteer holds up "Follow" Daily Mission Pennant or reproduction.* Leader *pauses as audience answers "FOLLOW in God's Path."*) It isn't always easy to follow God, but God will help us. (Leader *opens Bible and reads Jeremiah 7:23.*) This verse promises that things will go well if we follow in God's path. That doesn't mean it will always be easy or that we won't have any problems. But we can have courage because we know that God's in charge and He's got a path for us—the best possible path to follow!

Prayer

Leader: Dear God, thank You for loving us and making a path for each of us. Help us to have courage to always obey You. In Jesus' name, amen.

Song

(Leader *leads singing of "Be Strong and Courageous."*)

Announcements/ Dismissal

(Leader *explains procedure for Session 4 and dismisses students to classes.*)

Closing Assembly

Materials: See prop list on page 19.

Play songs from CD as children gather. Give "Follow" Daily Mission Pennant or reproduction to a volunteer to hold up during assembly.

Song

Leader: Let's sing our song about obeying God! (Leader *leads singing of "Obey Me."*)

Prizes

(Leader *distributes Star Prize(s) [for more information, see p. 6]*.)

Review

Leader: I sure have had a lot of fun today at the SonForce Agency! Did you have fun, too? (Leader *pauses for response. Volunteer holds up "Follow" Daily Mission Pennant or reproduction.*) **What is today's Daily Mission?** (Leader *pauses as audience answers "FOLLOW in God's Path."*) **In today's Bible story, the king didn't want to hear God's warning. So he cut up the scroll. What did he do next to the scroll?** (Leader *pauses as audience answers "Burned it."*) **Even though the king didn't want to obey God, we saw that Jeremiah obeyed God— even when it was hard! Let's say today's Bible Memory Verse together.** (Leader *guides audience in reciting Jeremiah 7:23 aloud.*) **It can be hard to obey God when we feel angry or tired, or when everyone else is disobeying God. But our verse reminds us that the best way to go is to follow God—in everything we do!**

Prayer

Leader: Dear God, please help us to always choose to follow You. We love You. In Jesus' name, amen.

Announcements/ Dismissal

Leader: (Leader *makes announcements and invites children back for the next session. Felton enters and stands next to* Leader.) **Come back (tomorrow) when we'll hear Felton say:**

Felton: (*Frantically.*) **It's no joke! I can't stop the asteroid!**

Leader: Oh, no! That sounds serious! Come back tomorrow and see if our SonForce friends find a way to stop that asteroid! We'll also hear about a time two men stayed courageous, even though others around them were afraid.

Session Five

5 LEAD
Others to God's Promises

Opening Assembly/Skit

Materials: See prop list on page 19.

Preparation: To prepare for the **Stunt**, set whiteboard at center of stage. Place dry-erase markers beside whiteboard. Draw four blank lines on the whiteboard, one for each letter of the key word from the Daily Mission, "LEAD." In each pie plate, place five plastic insects. Fill plate with whipped cream and cover insects. Cover Center Console or table with plastic tablecloth or bedsheet and place filled plates on top.

There is no special preparation for the **Bible Story Preview**.

To prepare for the **Assembly Skit**, set stage and prepare actors as directed in "Skit Setup" (see p. 17). Cue "Confession Video" from Session 2 skit to be projected onto large screen. Cue "Red Alert" sound effect to play from *SonForce Kids CD*.

Play songs from CD as children gather. Give "Lead" Daily Mission Pennant or reproduction to a volunteer to hold up during assembly.

Welcome

Leader: Today's our last day at the SonForce Agency. If you're excited about being here, jump up and down, pump your fists in the air and shout "SonForce!" (*Enthusiastically guides everyone to respond several times.*) **We've learned a lot about courage and serving God! Today we're going to discover ways we can LEAD Others to God's Promises.**

Song

Leader: Let's start off by singing one of my favorite SonForce songs. Let's sing "God's Kids"! (*Leads singing of "God's Kids."*)

Stunt

Stunt Performers: Select four adult volunteers (VBS director, activity leader, church pastor, etc.).

Stunt Action: Give each volunteer a whipped-cream-filled plate. Volunteers take turns using their teeth to catch the plastic insects in their plates. When the first volunteer finds an insect, he or she calls on someone in the audience to guess a letter of the alphabet. If the letter guessed is in the word "lead," the letter is written on the correct line on the whiteboard and the next volunteer takes his or her turn. If an incorrect letter is guessed, the volunteer returns to the pie plate and tries to catch another insect. If a volunteer finds all the insects in his or her plate before a correct letter is guessed, give him or her the extra plate. Use towels for cleanup as needed. Continue until all four letters have been guessed.

Bible Story Preview

Improvisation Performers: Two adults dressed in black suits, with white shirts, black ties and dark sunglasses.

Improvisation: Instead of using names, actors refer to each other by their initials. The agent who learned to follow on the day before is now showing what he or she learned by surreptitiously following the other agent through the audience and up to the stage. The first agent is unaware of his or her presence until reaching center stage when the following agent suddenly jumps forward and yells. The first agent is initially startled and then congratulatory. He or she then tells the other agent that the lesson on following was well learned and now it's time for him or her to learn to lead by leading audience in a quick game of Simon Says. (Play game so that no one is eliminated.) After a few minutes of playing Simon Says, agents end game and tell audience that leading people isn't as easy as it seems and that in today's Bible story they'll discover how two men, Joshua and Caleb, were leaders.

At the end of the improvisation, the Leader comes forward and speaks to the audience. **When we LEAD Others to God's Promises, we help them learn to be SonForce agents, too! Your mission today is to find out how you can have courage to lead others.**

Skit Script

Leader: (*Looking around at audience.*) **Well, I see everyone's ready for the big moment. Felton is ready to show everyone the satellite "bounce-back"! Let's see what happens!** (*Exits stage right.*)

(Felton *and* Miss Newton *enter from stage left. Red lights flash on and off three or four times. Play "Red Alert" sound effect. Immediately after, a robotic voice is heard from offstage: "Asteroid impact in 15 minutes.*")

Miss Newton: Goodness! That's awfully close!

Felton: Don't worry, Miss Newton, everything is under control—remote control, that is. (*He laughs and holds up his remote control.*)

Miss Newton: Oh, Edward! (*She laughs and pats him on the shoulder. Then she turns to the audience.*) **Attention, everyone! I'm so glad you are able to be here. In just a few moments, Edward here will save us all!** (*She motions everyone to applaud as* Felton *bows.*) **Edward, please explain to everyone what will happen.**

Felton: Thank you! Thank you! If you will all simply watch the monitor, you'll see the asteroid as it barrels closer to the SonForce Agency Satellite Station. (*On large screen, play "Confession Video" from Session 2 skit.*) **In just a moment, I'll use my remote control to activate the . . .** (*He sees what the video is showing.* Inez, Jack *and* Robot *enter from stage right.*) **Oh, no!** (*He hurriedly sticks remote in a pocket and starts to run off stage right, but seeing the others, realizes he has no escape. He stands dejected, as video plays.*)

Miss Newton: (*At end of video.*) **Edward! I'm so disappointed in you!**

Robot: (*Turning to* Miss Newton.) **My emotional sensors tell me that you are both surprised and disappointed. We're sorry to have to spring the news this way, but we barely had time to intercept the transmission.**

Inez: Jack, I think you'd better explain to Miss Newton what just happened.

Jack: Robot has a video recorder installed in his optical processing unit. I overheard Felton telling Robot about his plan. I knew I could retrieve it from Robot's recorder if I could regain control of Robot. We figured the best way to prove Felton was behind the asteroid problem was for him to say so himself!

(Red lights flash on and off three or four times. Play "Red Alert" sound effect. Immediately after, a robotic voice is heard from offstage: "Asteroid impact in 10 minutes.")

Miss Newton: Oh, no!

Jack: Come on, Felton. Time to stop that asteroid before it hits!

Felton: Fine! (*As he pulls the remote from his pocket, he drops it.*) **Oops!** (*He picks up remote and pushes a button, then he frantically starts pushing all the buttons.*) **It's broken! The remote is not responding! I can't stop the asteroid!**

Miss Newton: Now is no time to joke, Edward.

Felton: It's no joke! I can't stop the asteroid! (*The seriousness of what he's done dawns on him.*) I can't believe how I messed up! I've risked all our lives just so everyone would think I was a hero! (*He drops remote and hangs his head in shame.* Inez *picks up remote, and running, takes it to* Jack *who starts looking it over.*)

(*Red lights flash on and off three or four times. Play "Red Alert" sound effect. Immediately after, a robotic voice is heard from offstage: "Asteroid impact in five minutes. All hands to Red Alert." Play "Asteroid" sound effect.*)

Miss Newton: (*Panicked.*) **What will we do?** (Jack, *who has been looking over the remote, shakes his head and shrugs as if to say he doesn't know how to fix it.*)

Inez: Come on, Jack. Don't give up! There must be SOMETHING we can do!

Jack: Inez, that remote is TOASTED. There's no way I can fix it in time.

Robot: Maybe there's a way I can help.

Inez: Sure! Come on, Jack, think! Isn't there something in Robot's database?

Jack: (*An idea has formed.*) Robot, did you help Felton with any of his research?

Robot: Edward Clark Felton researched asteroids on my database. He also input navigational and descriptive information about the asteroid in question.

Inez: (*Catching on.*) And do you still have the algorithms I programmed into you for calculating navigational maps?

Robot: That programming remains intact.

Jack: And your basic programming on force fields?

Robot: (*Walks over to central console and begins making adjustments using keyboard, mouse and any buttons or levers that may be there.*) Yes. I see what you and Inez are saying. From the information and programs you mentioned, I will extrapolate the signal necessary to stop this asteroid with a force field from the satellite station tower.

Felton: Of course! (*Smacks himself upside the head.*) Why didn't I think of that?

Miss Newton: What is the robot saying? What does it mean?

Jack: He's saying he can REALLY do what Felton PRETENDED to do! He's going to use the tower to send out a bounce-back beam!

(*Play "Alert/Bounce-Back" sound effect. Immediately after "Alert" portion of sound effect, a robotic voice is heard from offstage: "Asteroid impact in two minutes. All hands to Red Alert." Red light continues turning on and off.*)

Miss Newton: Do it! Do it!

Inez: Go, Robot! (*All wait in anticipation, listening until they hear the "BOING!" portion of sound effect. Red light stays off.*)

Jack: That's it, Robot! You did it! (*He pats* Robot *on the back.*)

Miss Newton and Inez: Hooray! (*They jump and clap.*)

Felton: Good work, you guys! (*He walks over to* Inez *and* Jack *and shakes their hands.*)

Miss Newton: Inez, Jack . . . I owe the two of you an apology. I should have believed you when you told me about Edward's fooling us. And I'm sorry you were made Level 1 agents, when it obviously wasn't your fault the robot took off my . . . (*Stops and pats her hair.*) Oh, well, you all know what happened. Inez and Jack, you are both hereby moved up to Level 5! (*She beams with pride.*)

Inez: Thanks, Miss Newton! We're glad to move up to Level 5 if that means we can be of greater service.

Jack: Now I know it's more important to do the right thing than to try to impress people.

Felton: You know, I've been so concerned about making people THINK I was a hero, I didn't realize if I DID the right thing, I WOULD be a hero.

Miss Newton: Oh, yes . . . Mr. Felton . . . as for you— (*She reaches behind console to pull out bucket and toilet brush.*)

Felton: I think I know . . . Level 1, huh? (*He takes the bucket and brush.*) Well, Inez and Jack learned a lot by being Level 1 agents, maybe I will, too!

Robot: Jack? Remember when you said I could choose my own name? Have I earned the right yet?

Jack: Oh, you bet! So what is your name going to be?

Robot: I think I'd like to be called "Robert."

Jack: "Robert the Robot"?

Robot: No, just Robert. And, Miss Newton, I'd like to be a SonForce agent, too. What do you say?

Miss Newton: I say "Welcome to SonForce Agency, Robert!" (*All laugh and exit stage right.*)

Leader: (*Enters from stage right.*) Wow! That was exciting, wasn't it? It's a good thing they were able to stop the asteroid in time. And it seems Edward Felton learned what it really means to be a hero.

Edward learned about being a hero by watching what Inez and Jack did, and listening to what they said. Our friends and family will watch and listen to us, too. As SonForce agents, we can lead others to learn about God and His promises by the things that we do and say.

Bible Memory Verse

Leader: What is our Daily Mission today? (*Volunteer holds up "Lead" Daily Mission Pennant or reproduction. Leader pauses as audience answers "LEAD Others to God's Promises."*) Today we're going to talk about the ways knowing and believing in God's promises can help us. And if they help us, they'll help other people, too! God wants us to lead others to His promises. (*Leader opens Bible and reads Joshua 1:9.*) It isn't always easy to lead others or to talk to them about God, but knowing God is with us wherever we go can give us all the courage we need!

Prayer

Leader: Dear God, thank You for giving us courage and for being with us wherever we go. Please help us to lead others to believe in You and Your great promises. In Jesus' name, amen.

Song

(*Leader leads singing of "Be Strong and Courageous."*)

Announcements/ Dismissal

(*Leader explains procedure for Session 5 and dismisses students to classes.*)

Closing Assembly

Materials: See prop list on page 19.

Play songs from CD as children gather. Give "Lead" Daily Mission Pennant or reproduction to a volunteer to hold up during assembly.

Song

Leader: Let's sing our song about our mission of love! (Leader *leads singing of "Mission of Love."*)

Prizes

(Leader *distributes Star Prize(s) [for more information, see p. 6].*)

Review

Leader: What a wonderful time we've had at the SonForce Agency! Are you glad you became SonForce Kids special agents? (Leader *pauses for response. Volunteer holds up "Lead" Daily Mission Pennant or reproduction.*) What was today's Daily Mission? (Leader *pauses as audience answers "LEAD Others to God's Promises."*) In today's Bible story, who said the Israelites should trust in God's promises and tried to lead them into the Promised Land? (Leader *pauses as audience answers "Joshua and Caleb."*) Let's say today's Bible Memory Verse together. (Leader *guides audience in reciting Joshua 1:9 aloud.*) This is one of the many promises of help that God gives us in the Bible. When it seems too hard to lead others or we're feeling discouraged, God will help us by giving us the courage we need.

Prayer

Leader: Dear God, we love You! Thank You for always being with us and giving us the courage we need to lead others to You. In Jesus' name, amen.

Announcements/ Dismissal

Remind children to invite their parents and friends to the Closing Program. Children take home all projects and materials.

Closing Program

Performance Preparation

As you prepare the Closing Program, work closely with the Special Events Coordinator and the Music Director.

>> The Special Events Coordinator will organize all aspects of the Closing Program.

>> The Music Director will make sure children know the songs to be performed during the skit.

>> Preschoolers and kindergartners learn words and actions of "Be Strong and Courageous" and "Listen to Advice."

>> Elementary children learn words and motions of "Be Strong and Courageous," "I Trust You With My Life," "Together in Harmony," "Train Me Up," "Obey Me!" "Mission of Love" and "God's Kids."

>> Elementary children learn the optional songs "Come Together and Unite" and/or "Listen to Advice." These optional songs may be sung during a slide or video show or as indicated in the Skit Script.

>> Photocopy the Skit Script (pp. 48-50) and give a copy to each actor in the skit. Rehearse actors alone and then rehearse entire production with all children before the actual performance.

The Closing Program is written using characters from the assembly skits. If you did not choose the assembly skits as part of your assemblies, consider one of the Stunts and/or Bible Story Previews. You might choose to repeat a favorite or feature one that you didn't do during VBS.

Stage Set

Use the Mission Command Backdrop. Place Center Console at downstage center. On top, place a computer setup at each end.

Characters

The Closing Program uses the same skit characters as the other skits: Miss Newton, Felton, Inez, Jack and Robot. These characters are described in detail on pages 8-9.

Kid Agents 1, 2, 3, 4, 5, 6, 7 and 8 have just one or two lines. Assign these parts to your most enthusiastic VBS kids!

Props

See prop list on page 19.

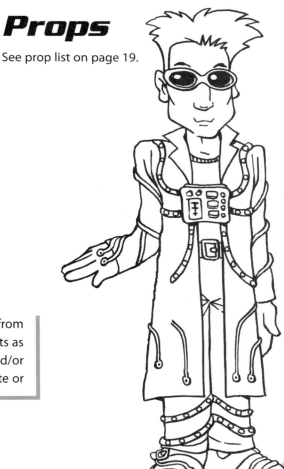

Skit Script

Play *SonForce Kids CD* as children and parents gather.

Leader: Welcome to the Closing Program of SonForce Kids! As you can see, our church has been transformed into Mission Command at the SonForce Agency's satellite station. Here at the SonForce Agency, your children have learned about having courage to serve God. Now we'd like to share more with you about what we've done!

Slide/Video Presentation [Optional]

Leader: We'd like to show you some of what we've discovered here at the SonForce Agency.

(*Show slides or a videotape of activities that took place during VBS. Play songs from* SonForce Kids *CD or have children sing optional songs during the presentation.*)

Stunt [Optional]

If you have been using the stunts provided for each day's assembly, you may wish to repeat a favorite stunt during your Closing Program.

Scene 1

(*Play "SonForce Logo Animation" from* The Asteroid Incident Skit DVD.)

Miss Newton: (*Enters from stage right.* Felton, Inez, Jack *and* Robot *follow. All cross to center.*) **Hello, and welcome to Mission Command here at SonForce Agency's satellite station. I'm glad to see so many of you VIPs** (*Indicates audience.*) **made the journey from Earth to be here with us tonight. I'm Miss Newton, the head of SonForce Agency, and here are some of our agents:** (*Indicates each character as she says his or her name. Actors raise hands when their character is named.*) **Edward Clark Felton, Inez Halley, Jack Oort and Robot** (Robot *clears his*

throat and looks meaningfully at Miss Newton.) . . . **I mean ROBERT.** (Robot *nods, pleased.*) **I know you're all anxious to hear more about our training program for special agents. We'll be able to start as soon as the rest of our special agents join us. Oh! Here they come now!** (*Points in direction elementary and preschool children are entering from.*)

Elementary and preschool children sing "Be Strong and Courageous."

(*As they sing, elementary children file in and take their positions in front of and/or around sides of stage. Preschool children line up in front of elementary children. Be sure adult volunteers are on hand to help children get situated.*)

Scene 2

(*Preschool children sit down.*)

Jack: Boy, did we need courage this week!

Miss Newton: Yes, we did, Jack. (*To audience.*) You may have heard about the asteroid problem we had last week.

Inez: I think "problem" is putting it mildly! That asteroid was going to first smash this satellite station to smithereens and THEN it was going to crash right into Earth!

Felton: (*Attempting to mollify the situation.*) Well, it wasn't REALLY going to crash into anything—

Jack: Until you broke your remote!

Miss Newton: We're getting ahead of ourselves! In all difficult situations, it's important to remember that God has a plan!

Kid Agent 1: We can all TRUST in God's Plans. (Kid Agent 1 *holds up "Trust" Daily Mission Pennant or reproduction.*) God loves us and we can trust Him with our lives!

Elementary children sing "I Trust You with My Life."

Inez: Trusting God is a good thing to do. But it isn't always an EASY thing to do.

Robot: In difficult situations, it can help to have someone working with you. I wouldn't be able to perform a simple arithmetic problem if it weren't for the programming Inez and Jack gave me.

Jack: Yeah! And I know I need Inez as my partner lots of times. Not just to accomplish a mission, but because it gives me courage to have a partner with me.

Kid Agent 2: We can do great things when we UNITE with God's People! (Kid Agent 2 *holds up "Unite" Daily Mission Pennant or reproduction.*)

Elementary children sing "Together in Harmony."

(Optional: Elementary children sing "Come Together and Unite.")

Scene 3

Felton: Hmm . . . Maybe if I'd had a partner, I would not have tried so hard to prove I was a hero.

Miss Newton: Yes, Edward. That led you to do things you later regretted, didn't it? (*Felton nods.*) I think it's time you told our guests your involvement with the asteroid problem.

Felton: (*Steps forward. Clears his throat and then looks back at others obviously a bit afraid. They motion encouragingly for him to go on. He nods and then speaks.*) It's because of me that there WAS an asteroid problem. (*Speaks a little faster now that he's started. Wants to get everything out.*) You see, I came up with this idea to set an asteroid on a collision course with Earth. I made it so that I could control the asteroid with a remote control. I knew if I stopped it, everyone would think I was a HERO! But then Jack found out, so I tied him and Inez up in the bathroom . . . Oh, yeah, that was AFTER I took control of their robot and made him obey me . . . And then I broke the remote control and we were in REALLY BIG trouble 'cause I couldn't stop the asteroid anymore and . . . and . . . and . . . (*He's winding down.*) It was just a really DUMB idea.

(*Preschool children stand.*)

Miss Newton: Our youngest group of agents have a song about how not to be dumb . . . Or rather, how to be wise!

Preschool children sing "Listen to Advice."

(Optional: Elementary children sing along.)

Scene 4

(*An offstage voice is heard, "All agents with Preschool or Kindergarten classification are to report immediately to the holodeck for training. Please exit in an orderly fashion." Preschool children exit.*)

Felton: "Listen to advice and accept instruction" . . . That's something I'd better do if I want to work my way up to being a Level 5 agent.

Jack: I'm just glad you're planning to WORK your way to Level 5 instead of FAKING it again.

Felton: You're right. I was all mixed-up about that. I definitely need some more training before I take on any important missions.

Miss Newton: Training is very important! That's why the SonForce Agency is here: not just to assign missions, but to properly equip special agents for those missions.

Kid Agent 3: At SonForce Kids, we TRAIN for God's Service! (Kid Agent 3 *holds up "Train" Daily Mission Pennant or reproduction.*)

Elementary children sing "Train Me Up."

Miss Newton: Good training is all about learning to make WISE CHOICES. It doesn't make you blindly obey as if you were a robot. (*Turning to Robot.*) No offense intended!

Robot: No offense taken! I'm lucky to have artificial-intelligence components that allow me to compare alternatives and choose the best option. I've only had to blindly obey once—and that was when Felton took control of my central processing unit. (*All look at* Felton.)

Felton: (*Sheepishly.*) Yeah . . . I'm sorry about that!

Inez: God doesn't want us to blindly obey Him. That's why He made us so that we can make choices.

Kid Agent 4: God wants us to make the wise choice to FOLLOW in His Path. (Kid Agent 4 *holds up "Follow" Daily Mission Pennant or reproduction.*)

Elementary children sing "Obey Me!"

Felton: That makes a lot of sense. God is more wise and powerful than anyone! So His path has gotta be the best possible path for us to follow!

Jack: Not just us—EVERYONE! God has a path for everyone. That's what the Bible tells us.

Miss Newton: The Bible is full of God's promises. What are some of God's promises?

Inez: God loves us!

Kid Agent 5: God is with us everywhere!

Robot: God forgives!

Jack: God hears our prayers!

Kid Agent 6: God gives us courage!

Felton: And these promises are for everyone? That's fantastic!

Kid Agent 7: We can LEAD Others to God's Promises! (Kid Agent 7 *holds up "Lead" Daily Mission Pennant or reproduction.*)

Miss Newton: The most important promise from God is the promise that we can become members of His family. God's Son, Jesus, had the most important mission in the history of the earth: Making a way for us to be members of God's family.

Elementary children sing "Mission of Love."

Inez: I'm glad that as SonForce Kids special agents, we can tell others about Jesus' great mission.

Miss Newton: That's what being a SonForce Kids special agent is all about.

Robot: I can't wait to begin my training!

Felton: I'm really glad I learned a lot about what being a special agent for God REALLY means!

Kid Agent 8: Being SonForce Kids special agents means we're all God's kids!

Elementary children sing "God's Kids."

Skit characters stand and join in singing song and doing motions.

Closing

Leader or minister thanks parents for coming and invites them to learn more about God and His Son, Jesus, by attending other events of the church family. Invite everyone to enjoy the refreshments (in the fellowship hall, on the lawn, etc.) and try to meet at least one other family they didn't know before. Dismiss with a brief prayer of gratitude.

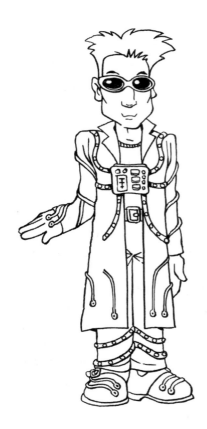

Bible Story Skits

Bring Bible Stories to Life!

Drama activities are valuable learning opportunities because of the process experienced by group members, not because of the quality of the final performance. Bible stories come alive when acted out, and Bible truth is seen to be relevant when applied to contemporary situations. In addition:

>> Acting out a situation will push students to think about the application of Bible truth to a real-life circumstance.

>> Dramatic activities provide a unique opportunity to briefly step into another person's shoes and experience some of his or her attitudes and feelings.

Ways to Use Bible Story Skits in Your VBS

>> Instead of telling the story as written in the *Preteen Bible Story Center Guide,* ask preteen students to perform the skits for their own classes or for children in younger grades.

>> Ask older students and/or youth helpers to present the Bible story skits as a review during a 10-day VBS (see suggested schedule in *Director's Guide*).

>> Present one or more skits as part of your Closing Program.

Getting Ready

After you've chosen and reproduced copies of the skit for the participants, here are some tips for preparing to present the skit:

>> Read the Scripture passage. Familiarize yourself with the corresponding Bible story as presented in any age-level *Bible Story Center Guide*.

>> Read the skit, noting any vocabulary or pronunciation help you will need to give your performers.

>> Adapt the script if needed by reducing or increasing the number of characters, by adding a scene, etc.

>> Collect props.

Practical Tips

One of the nicest things about these Bible story skits is that they are easy to prepare. Skits are not big Broadway-type productions. They can be informal and spontaneous. They can be primped and polished to the hilt when the mood strikes. A lot or a little—it all depends on how you want to do it. Here are the basics:

>> Good acting is a plus, but it's not essential in order to have a positive experience. What is essential is that the lines are heard by the audience. The performers need to speak slowly and clearly—with their voices directed to the audience.

>> It is not necessary for performers to memorize the script. Reading works as well. Provide several highlighter pens for performers to mark their parts. You may give out the script ahead of time for the performers to practice. However, if you hand out the scripts ahead of time, bring extra copies on performance day, because someone will undoubtedly forget his or her copy.

>> Practicing the skits ahead of time will be most important for younger groups and groups for whom English is a second language.

>> Though not necessary, Bible-times costumes add a nice touch for Bible-times characters.

>> Optional: Make signs printed with the setting of each scene. Have a volunteer hold up signs to announce the change of scene.

Moses: Boy in a Basket

Materials: See prop list on page 19.

Preparation: Set finished basket off stage right. Hand unfinished basket and reeds to Mother.

Characters

Father: An Israelite father

Mother: An Israelite mother

Miriam: Their daughter

Princess: Pharaoh's daughter

Maid 1: Maid of Princess

Maid 2: Maid of Princess

Maid 3: Maid of Princess

Narrator

Script

Scene 1: Home of Moses' family.

Narrator: Our story begins in ancient Egypt, near the Banks of the Nile River. The Egyptian Pharaoh is worried that the Israelites he keeps as slaves will one day rise up and take over. So he has issued a terrible order: Kill all the Israelite baby boys! But one brave family has kept their infant son hidden for three months.

(Father *paces frantically;* Mother *calmly weaves a basket.*)

Father: This can't go on any longer. I can't take the stress.

Mother: The stress?

Father: Yes, the stress! Will the baby cry? Will Pharaoh's soldiers hear?

Mother: Oh, THAT stress.

Father: Yes! That stress! Hiding him here is the WORST plan ever! Something must be done!

Mother: I agree.

Father: I don't believe this. I'm going crazy and you're sitting there, calmly weaving reeds. What are you weaving?

Mother: A basket.

Father: What for? We're slaves. We don't have enough of ANYTHING to put in such a big basket.

Mother: On the contrary. We have something very important to put in this basket. Our son.

Father: You think that basket will keep him safe? The stress has made you even crazier than I am!

Mother: I'm not crazy. Look, we can't keep him quiet forever. Sooner or later, Pharaoh's men will hear him.

Father: And when they find we have a baby boy, they'll kill us AND him.

Mother: But what if they don't find a baby here? What if instead of trusting in our ability to hide the baby, we trust God instead?

Father: Isn't that what we've been doing?

Mother: Yes . . . but not fully. Here's my plan. I weave a basket.

Father: To stay busy?

Mother: Listen! I cover it with tar to make it waterproof and put the baby inside.

Father: So the baby won't get wet when it rains?

Mother: No. So it will float on the river.

Father: Float on the river! Where do you plan for it to go?

Mother: That's up to God. We simply trust that God has a plan for the baby.

Father: And I thought the OTHER plan was bad . . . IF the basket doesn't sink, and IF the crocodiles don't get him, it's only a matter of time before Pharaoh's men find him and kill him!

Mother: Don't you think we can trust God with our baby?

Father: (*Reluctantly.*) Okay, maybe you're right. But I'm likely to go crazy, not knowing what will happen to our son.

Mother: So would I. But I have an idea.

Father: What is it?

Mother: Our daughter Miriam can help me take the basket to the river. Then she will hide, see what happens and come home to tell us.

Father: Well, at least we'll know what happens to him. But it's so . . . difficult.

Scene 2: Nile River.

Narrator: Later that day, a young girl hides in the reeds, anxiously waiting to see what will happen to her baby brother.

Miriam: (*To herself.*) Miriam, keep that baby quiet! Miriam, get me some reeds! Miriam, watch over that baby in the basket! Watch him do WHAT? Get captured by Pharaoh's men, or eaten by crocodiles? (*Sees* Princess *and* Maids *approaching.*) Oh, no! Pharaoh's daughter!

Princess: Ooooh! I can't wait for a nice bath in the Nile! The squishy mud, the cool water . . .

Maid 1: (*Whispering.*) The snapping crocodiles.

Maid 2: (*Whispering.*) The swirling currents.

Maid 3: (*Whispering.*) The biting insects.

Princess: What was that?

Maids: (*Together.*) Nothing, your highness!

Miriam: (*To herself.*) Maybe she won't see the basket!

Princess: (*Pointing off stage right.*) Is that a basket floating behind those reeds? Bring it here!

Maid 1: (*Crosses stage right, peering offstage.*) It's just a soggy old basket. Someone as wealthy and powerful as you must have THOUSANDS of baskets nicer than that one!

Miriam: (*To herself.*) Okay, she's SEEN the basket. But maybe she won't want it!

Princess: I said, "Bring it here!"

Miriam: (*To herself.*) Okay, so she WANTS the basket. But maybe she won't open it? Maybe the baby won't cry?

(Maid 1 *picks up basket and brings it to the* Princess.)

Princess: (*Opening basket.*) Look! It's a baby! And he's crying! (Miriam *shrugs and rolls her eyes.*)

Maid 1: (*Sticking fingers in ears.*) He sure has a good set of lungs on him!

Princess: Poor little guy must be hungry. (*Hands basket to* Maid 1.) Nurse him!

Maid 1: But I haven't had a baby. I can't nurse him! (*Hands basket to* Maid 2.) Here, YOU nurse him.

Maid 2: I can't nurse him, either. (*Hands basket to* Maid 3.) Here, YOU nurse him.

Maid 3: Well, I can't nurse him, either!

Miriam: (*To herself.*) Oh, brother! (*Stepping out of reeds.*) Um, your highness? Um . . . I could . . . if you wanted—

Princess: Speak up, girl! What is it?

Miriam: Would you like me to find an Israelite woman to nurse the baby for you?

Princess: Yes, go!

Narrator: A short time later, Miriam returns with her mother.

Miriam: This lady says she'd be happy to help you with the baby!

Princess: (*Handing baby to* Mother.) Take this baby and nurse him for me, and I will pay you.

Mother: Yes, your highness! I will!

(Miriam *and* Mother *walk away, carrying the baby and the basket.*)

Miriam: Mother, that was the BEST plan!

Mother: Trusting God is ALWAYS the best plan, Miriam.

Esther: Queen at Risk

Materials: See prop list on page 19.

Preparation: Place some toy food on the large platter. Place table at stage left. Use table decorations and remaining toy food to decorate table. Hand long sheet of paper and thin stick to Esther.

Characters:

Servant: Queen Esther's female servant

Esther: Queen of Persia

Xerxes (ZERK-sees)**:** King of Persia

Haman (HAY-mahn)**:** King Xerxes's right-hand man

Script

Scene 1: A corridor in the Persian palace of King Xerxes.

Servant: (*Enters stage right carrying large platter of food.*) Go here. Do that. Dust this. Bring that. That's all I hear. One big fancy dinner for the king wasn't enough for Esther. Oh, no! She's got to have TWO big fancy dinners. Two nights in a row! You know, I could have been queen, instead of her. I was one of the women chosen to meet the king so he could choose the one who pleased him most. If King Xerxes had chosen me instead of Esther, I'd be queen! (*Exits stage left in a huff.*)

Esther: (*Enters stage right using thin stick as a pen as if checking items off long sheet of paper.*) Meat cooked. CHECK! Table set. CHECK! Fruit washed. CHECK! (*Fluffs hair.*) Beautification done. CHECK! (*To audience.*) Everything's GOT to be perfect! Imagine if Mordecai (MOR-dih-ki) hadn't warned me that Haman is trying to have all the Jewish people in the kingdom destroyed, including Mordecai—and even me! But like Mordecai says, maybe THIS is the rea-

son God made me queen. I'm so glad that for the last three days, the Jewish people have united with me in prayer and fasting. With their support, I know I'll be able to stand up for them. May God be with us! (*Exits stage left.*)

Xerxes: (*Enters stage right.*) I wonder what it is that Queen Esther wants. It must be something very important for her to have risked her life coming to see me uninvited. And now she's invited me to dinner, not once but twice! Hmm . . . (*Exits stage left.*)

Servant: (*Enters stage left.*) Fix this. Fetch that. I'll be exhausted before the night is through. You know, I could have been queen . . . (*Exits stage right.*)

Haman: (*Enters stage right.*) I am the second most important man in the kingdom. You want proof? Last night, the queen had a private banquet; today, she's having another. Do you know who was invited? The king and I were. That's all. No princes, no foreign royalty. I would be the happiest man in the world if it weren't for that Mordecai. But I have plans to take care of him! (*Exits stage left.*)

Scene 2: The banquet room in Queen Esther's chambers.

Xerxes: (*Leaning back from the table, contentedly.*) Queen Esther, that was a magnificent meal you prepared.

Esther: Thank you, my king.

Servant: (*To herself while clearing away dishes.*) Meal SHE prepared. I'll tell you who did all the work—ME.

Xerxes: Don't you think it was a great meal, Haman?

Haman: My most mighty king, ruler of Medes and Persia, may you live forever, may I say that I am honored to even be dining with you.

Xerxes: A simple "Yes" will do.

Haman: Of course, my most excellent king, conqueror of the known world . . .

Xerxes: Yeah, yeah, thanks, Haman.

Servant: (*To herself while continuing to clean.*) I have no idea why Esther would invite that pompous windbag, Haman, to her dinner. I wouldn't have, if I were queen, which I COULD have been . . .

Xerxes: My beautiful queen, the dinners last night and tonight have been wonderful. But I know there's something on your mind. Whatever it is that you want, you can have it.

Servant: Anything she wants? Even, say, if she asked for half of your kingdom?

Xerxes: Yes, you impudent servant, even if she asked for half of my kingdom.

Esther: All I ask, my gracious king, is for my life and for the lives of my people.

Xerxes: That's it? Well, of course you can have that. Don't you already have it?

Esther: My king, a death sentence has been issued against my people.

Xerxes: Death sentence? I don't remember issuing a death sentence against you.

Haman: (*Gets up to leave.*) Well, uh . . . I'd better be going. Have to get home to the wife and kids, you know.

Xerxes: Sit down; I may need your help and advice.

Haman: (*Sitting down.*) Of course, my king, may you live forever. (*Whispers.*) Or for no more than 30 seconds, if I'm lucky.

Esther: My king, a man you trust tricked you into issuing a death sentence against me and all my people. All because he has a grudge against my cousin Mordecai.

Haman: (*To himself.*) Mordecai's her cousin? That means she's Jewish! Oh, great! (*Standing and speaking to all.*) Pardon me, O mighty ruler, but I really must be going . . .

Xerxes: Sit down! (Haman *sits.* Xerxes *turns to* Esther.) Who would DARE to threaten my beloved queen?! Who is this man?

Esther: (*Pointing to* Haman.) It's Haman. He wanted the death of my people.

Xerxes: (*To* Haman.) Now I understand why you wanted to leave, you vile snake.

Haman: Your majesty, I can explain . . .

Xerxes: Haman, you are finished!

Haman: Finished?! Surely your majesty doesn't mean . . . Look . . . it was all a mistake . . . (Xerxes *drags* Haman *offstage left.*)

Servant: Whoa! That was intense! I'm sure glad I'm not queen! (*Exits stage right.*)

Esther: (*As she exits stage left, she calls offstage.*) Mordecai! Mordecai! I have great news! Our people are safe! God has helped us once again!

Session 3 Bible Story Skit

Daniel: Man of God

Materials: None.

Preparation: None.

Characters

Daniel: A teenage Israelite boy, who has just been taken captive by the Babylonians

Meshach (MEE-shahk)**:** Daniel's friend, also a teenage Israelite boy

Shadrach (SHAHD-rahk)**:** Daniel's friend, also a teenage Israelite boy

Abednego (uh-BED-nee-goh): Daniel's friend, also a teenage Israelite boy

Scene: Royal rooms in Babylon.

Abednego: (*Looking around.*) You know, this isn't half bad.

Meshach: Sure, if you don't count the fact that we're PRISONERS of the Babylonians, miles away from our homes, with some dumb new foreign names, it's great!

Shadrach: Yeah, WE got foreign names, and that's what everyone remembers. But did you guys notice Daniel is still known by his Hebrew name?

Abednego: That's a good point . . . Why does he get to go down in history with his Hebrew name, and we get remembered by these dumb Babylonian names: (*Pointing to each in turn.*) Shadrach, Meshach, Abednego . . .

Meshach: Is that really what's important here?

Abednego: Hey, I'm just saying . . .

Shadrach: Guys! Let's not argue about it.

Abednego: You're right. No point in arguing about having new names. I mean, I can definitely see some positive aspects to our situation. Meshach, do you really think this is all that bad?

Meshach: YES! I can't believe we're even discussing this!

Shadrach: Yeah, but did you expect THIS when they dragged us away from home?

Meshach: I expected to end up dead! And that still might happen, if we're not careful.

Shadrach: We could have been made slaves like most of the other captives. Instead, we got selected to go into training for three years to serve the Babylonian king.

Abednego: Exactly! Look at all these books! This is a great library!

Meshach: Too bad we don't read the language.

Shadrach: They said they're going to teach us the language.

Abednego: Yeah. They're going to train us to be leaders!

Meshach: BABYLONIAN leaders. We were leaders at home! We were the smartest kids around. Everyone said that.

Abednego: True. Well, we weren't smarter than Daniel.

Shadrach: Where is Daniel, anyway?

Abednego: He went to talk to that head guy—the one that gave us all those tests.

Meshach: (*Alarmed.*) What?

Shadrach: Talk to him about what? I hope he isn't complaining. Daniel had better be careful—we ALL had better be careful. I don't think these Babylonian guys are exactly kind and tolerant people.

Meshach: Which is why Daniel is in real danger!

Abednego: Daniel? In danger? I doubt it. He's too smart.

Shadrach: Why'd he go see the guy anyway?

Abednego: Something about changing the dinner menu.

Meshach: I KNEW it! We're all going to die!

Shadrach: What IS your problem?

Meshach: I heard one guy say the king commanded we be given food from his own table! He's going to be pretty angry if Daniel turns it down!

Daniel: (*Entering.*) Oh, good. You're all here.

Meshach: And we're happy to see you're still alive. Or is this a farewell visit?

Daniel: Huh?

Shadrach: Don't mind him. He's been doom and gloom ever since we left Jerusalem.

Daniel: I see. Anyway, I've discussed the food problem with the guy in charge.

Shadrach: Food problem? What food problem?

Daniel: Well, they were planning on serving us food from the king's table.

Meshach: Told you!

Shadrach: So why's that a problem? It probably tastes great!

Daniel: The king dedicates his food to one of his false gods.

Shadrach: Food is food, isn't it?

Daniel: Don't tell me you've already forgotten our laws?

Shadrach: Hard to forget our laws when I still have a knot on my head from Rabbi Levi's constant rapping. "Young man, you will recite those laws until they stick in your head." (Shadrach *knocks on* Meshach's *head in demonstration.*)

Meshach: Ow!

Daniel: (*Knocks on* Shadrach's *head.*) OK, "young man," tell us why we aren't supposed to eat meat dedicated to false gods.

Shadrach: (*Rubbing head.*) Because Rabbi Levi will rap on your head if you do.

Daniel: (*Knocks on* Shadrach's *head again.*) Wrong! Because we're not to worship, or have any part in worshiping, any gods other than the one, true God!

Abednego: So what did that official guy say?

Daniel: He said no way! The king would cut off his head if he let us starve.

Meshach: (*Alarmed.*) You were planning to let us STARVE?!

Daniel: (*Laughing.*) No, not at all! I asked that we be allowed to eat vegetables and drink water instead of eating the king's rich food and drinking his wine. But he thought we'd be sick if that was all we ate.

Abednego: (*Sadly.*) No meat?

Shadrach: So if he didn't go for your plan, why do you look so happy?

Daniel: After he turned us down, I went to the guard who brings us our food. I made a bargain with him.

Shadrach: What kind of a bargain?

Daniel: We eat nothing but vegetables for the next 10 days. If we're still strong and healthy, he'll let us keep eating only vegetables! Isn't that great?

Meshach: Whoa! Nothing but vegetables?

Abednego: (*Sadly.*) No meat?

Daniel: Nope! Just vegetables! We'll show them that following God's laws is good for us! Now I'm going to go work in the gardens!

(Meshach, Shadrach *and* Abednego *watch as* Daniel *exits.*)

Meshach: Eat nothing but vegetables? I don't think so!

Abednego: (*Sadly.*) No meat?

Shadrach: Daniel's right. If the king's meat violates God's laws, then we can do without it!

Meshach: (*Sadly.*) Nothing but vegetables?

Abednego: (*Sadly.*) No meat?

Shadrach: At least we get to eat. Maybe it won't be so bad.

(Abednego, Shadrach *and* Meshach *stare at each other a moment.*)

Meshach, Shadrach and Abednego: (*In unison.*) We wanna go home!

Jeremiah: Prophet in Trouble

Materials: See prop list on page 19.

Preparation: Place table at center stage. Place chairs next to table. Place long stick inside scroll and roll up. Place sticks in a pile at one side of stage. Crumple tissue paper and place on rocks to form flames. Hand scroll to Baruch. Hand plastic or other blunt knife to Jehoiakim.

Characters

Jeremiah: Prophet of God

Baruch (BEHR-uhk)**:** Jeremiah's secretary

Michaiah (mih-KY-ah)**:** Official in king's court

Official 1: Official in king's court

Official 2: Official in king's court

Official 3: Official in king's court

Jehoiakim (jeh-HOY-ah-kihm)**:** King of Judah

Narrator

Script

Scene 1: Jeremiah's House, Judah.

Narrator: (*Enters.*) **Long ago in the land of Judah, God's people were disobedient and disloyal to Him. Time after time, God sent prophets like Jeremiah to tell the people terrible things would happen if they kept disobeying God. But every time, they ignored Jeremiah and wanted to hurt him for telling them God's messages! So God gave Jeremiah a special assignment.**

(Jeremiah *and* Baruch *enter and take seats at table. Narrator steps to the side and watches silently.*)

Jeremiah: Baruch, my friend! God wants us to write down everything—ALL the messages He has given me.

Baruch: Everything?

Jeremiah: Everything. Maybe if God's people see all of His messages together, they'll finally get it.

Baruch: Oh, boy . . . (*Opens scroll and takes out a thin stick to use as reed pen.*) **Ready!**

Jeremiah: "My wrath will break out and burn like fire because of the evil you have

done. Flee for safety without delay!" (Baruch *pretends to write on scroll.*)

Scene 2: God's Temple.

Narrator: (*Steps forward.* Baruch *stands.* Jeremiah *exits.*) **When the scroll was finished, Baruch took it to the Temple and read it aloud for everyone to hear.** (Narrator *steps to the side and watches silently.*)

Baruch: (Michaiah *enters as* Baruch *reads from scroll.*) **Here are God's words for you, just as He told them to Jeremiah: "My wrath will break out and burn like fire because of the evil you have done."**

Michaiah: Oh, no! This doesn't sound good!

Baruch: (*Still reading.*) "Flee for safety without delay! For I am bringing disaster from the north, even terrible destruction."

Michaiah: Does it say anything about the king? Like maybe what a great king he is, and how he'll live forever?

Baruch: (*Still reading.*) "He will have the burial of a donkey—dragged away and thrown outside the gates of Jerusalem."

Michaiah: That's terrible! Please tell me that's all there is!

Baruch: Oh, no. There's more. Lots more!

Michaiah: I'll have to see what the king's scribe and officials have to say about this. (*All but* Narrator *exit.*)

Scene 3: Office of the King's Scribe.

Narrator: (*Steps forward.* Scribe *and* Officials *enter.*) **Meanwhile, in the office of the king's scribe, many officials were gathered.** (Narrator *steps to the side and watches silently.*)

Michaiah: (*Runs in, breathless.*) I have terrible news! Jeremiah's secretary, Baruch, has read God's words to us. If Jeremiah's right, we're toast!

Official 1: Uh-oh. The king will be furious! But we'd better tell him ourselves before someone else does!

Official 2: First let's find out exactly what Jeremiah's saying this time. The king will have our heads if we get this wrong!

Narrator: (*Steps forward.*) So they sent someone to find Baruch. (Official 3 *exits, and then immediately returns with* Baruch. Narrator *steps to the side and watches silently.*)

Michaiah: Go ahead. Read it.

Baruch: (*Opens scroll and reads.*) "My wrath will break out and burn like fire because of the evil you have done."

Michaiah: Read the part about the king!

Baruch: (*Reading.*) "He will have the burial of a donkey—dragged away and thrown outside the gates of Jerusalem."

Official 2: Oh, the king won't like that last part—not one little bit!

Official 3: Baruch, you and Jeremiah have to go into hiding! Don't tell anyone where you're going! Leave the scroll with me. (Baruch *hands scroll to* Official 3. *All but* Narrator *exit.*)

Scene 4: The King's Apartment.

Narrator: (*Steps forward.*) Meanwhile, the king was warming himself by the fire in his apartment. (Narrator *steps to the side and watches silently.*)

(Jehoiakim *enters and sits in a chair, warming himself in front of fire.* Officials *enter.*)

Jehoiakim: What brings you out on such a cold night?

Official 1: We've come with some important news! Jeremiah—

Jehoiakim: Him again? That man's been claiming something bad will happen as long as anyone can remember!

Official 2: Yes, your highness, but we really think you ought to hear this! It sure scared me when I heard it!

Jehoiakim: Alright, already! Let's hear it, then.

Official 3: Very well, sir. (*Reading scroll.*) "My wrath will break out and burn like fire because of the evil you have done."

Jehoiakim: Burn like fire? I'll show you what will burn like fire! (*Takes out knife. Grabs scroll, cuts off a section and throws it into fire.*) Burn, baby, burn! (*Hands scroll back to* Official 3.) Keep reading!

Official 1: (*Worried.*) Are you sure that's a good idea, your highness?

Jehoiakim: READ!

Official 3: (*Reading.*) "Flee for safety without delay! For I am bringing disaster from the north, even terrible destruction."

Jehoiakim: Oh, yeah? Give me that! (*Repeats grabbing, tearing and burning of scroll. Hands scroll back to* Official 3.) Read on!

Official 2: (*Nervously.*) Really, sir, do you HAVE to burn it? Maybe we could just hide it or something?

Jehoiakim: (*Angrily.*) Leave me alone or the scroll won't be the only thing burning! (*To* Official 3.) What does it say about me?

Official 3: (*Reading reluctantly.*) "He will have the burial of a donkey—dragged away and thrown outside the gates of Jerusalem."

Jehoiakim: The burial of a donkey? (*Grabs, cuts up and burns rest of scroll.* Officials *look horrified.*) We'll see who's going to be dragged away! Be gone, all of you! And send in my special guards! They won't sleep until Jeremiah has been captured!

Official 3: Yes, sir. (*All but* Narrator *exit.*)

Narrator: (*Steps forward.*) But the king's guards could not find Jeremiah and Baruch, because God had hidden them. But even in their hiding place, God had another assignment for them. God wanted them to rewrite the scroll Jehoiakim had burned. Not only that, but more warnings as well! And just as they'd done before, Jeremiah and Baruch did exactly what God told them. (Narrator *exits.*)

Joshua: Spy in a Strange Land

Materials: None.

Preparation: None.

Characters

Shammua (shah-MEW-ah)**:** Spy sent to Canaan

Igal (I-gahl)**:** Spy sent to Canaan

Palti (PAHL-tee)**:** Spy sent to Canaan

Nahbi (NAH-bee)**:** Spy sent to Canaan

Joshua: Spy sent to Canaan

Caleb: Spy sent to Canaan

Script

Scene 1: Field in Canaan, near Jericho.

(*All enter.*)

Shammua: (*Spooked.*) Whoa! Did you see the size of those guys?

Igal: (*Confused.*) What guys?

Palti: (*Also spooked.*) Did you see the size of those walls?

Igal: (*Confused. Looking from one to the other.*) What guys? What walls?

Nahbi: (*Also spooked.*) Did you see the size of the city?

Igal: What guys? What walls? What city?

Joshua: (*Enthusiastic and excited.*) Did you see the size of the vineyards?

Caleb: (*Also enthusiastic.*) And how about the grain? This really is the land of milk and honey!

Joshua: Definitely the Promised Land—it's everything God promised it would be!

Shammua: I don't remember anything about those big guys being in God's promise.

Palti: Or those walls.

Nahbi: Or that city.

Igal: (*Even more confused and with growing irritation.*) WHAT guys? WHAT walls? WHAT city?

Shammua: Igal, what kind of a spy are you if you can't see?

Igal: (*Defensively.*) Hey . . . Moses picked me as a spy, same as you! And he's been our leader for a long time, so he must have known what he was doing.

Nahbi: Unless, of course, you forgot to MENTION that you're blind as a bat!

Caleb: Leave him alone. He's a great cover. How many spies travel with blind companions?

Igal: (*Exasperated.*) I'm not blind!

Shammua: You'd have to be blind not to see that huge city over there.

Palti: (*Worried.*) It must hold thousands of people! (*Shudders.*) And all great warriors, from the looks of it!

Caleb: Looks can be deceiving. Are we supposed to believe only what we can see with our eyes, or are we supposed to believe in God?

Igal: (*Sadly.*) I just don't know what's going on anymore.

Joshua: Well, Igal, even if you're blind—

Igal: I'M NOT BLIND!

Joshua: OK, I'm sorry! Blind or not blind, you should be able to SMELL. Breathe deeply. What do you smell?

Igal: (*Sniffs.*) Hmm. Sweet grass, ripening grain, fresh fruit, healthy animals and fragrant honey.

Palti: (*Disdainfully.*) You can't smell healthy animals!

Igal: (*Defensively.*) Oh, yes, I can!

Shammua: It doesn't matter. With those monsters over there, there is no way we're going to be able to move here.

Igal: Monsters?!

Joshua: There are no monsters.

Caleb: (*Confidently.*) Don't forget; we've got God on our side!

Shammua: What can God do about all this? If it were just one city, maybe. But they've ALL looked like this!

Palti: Yeah. Remember those giants in Hebron? They made these guys look small!

Igal: (*Scared.*) What giants?

Joshua: (*Reassuringly.*) They weren't really giants. They were just some very tall people.

Nahbi: They were GIANTS! And there's no way we can defeat them!

Joshua: If God could help us escape from Egypt, the most powerful country in the world, can't He help us here? Didn't he send us food to eat? Water to drink? Hasn't God PROVED His power over and over again?

Caleb: With such a wonderful, powerful and loving God on our side, can't we believe in His promise to give us this land?

Joshua: Yeah! With our belief in God making us strong, can't we just walk right into the land?

Nahbi, Palti and Shammua: (*Look at each other for a moment, considering. Then speaking in unison.*) Uh . . . NO!

Joshua: (*Incredulous.*) No?!

Caleb: Why not?

Shammua: Take a really good look at the walls around Jericho. (*Points offstage.*) Go ahead. LOOK at those walls! See how tall they are? See how big those stones are? See how tightly cemented they are? Those walls are so big and strong, there are men WALKING around on top of them! What's God going to do? Knock the walls down?

Joshua: He might.

Palti: Get a grip, Joshua!

Joshua: You know, Igal can see some things better than you, and he's blind!

Igal: I'm NOT blind!

Joshua: And NONE of you are listening!

Caleb: C'mon, Joshua. Let's go get some fruit to take back to Moses. When the people see how great it is, they'll know God keeps His promises. I saw a bunch of grapes so big it would take TWO of us to carry it back to the camp. (*Joshua and Caleb exit.*)

Nahbi: Those two are going to get us all killed!

Igal: I don't understand.

Shammua: What don't you understand?

Igal: Well, obviously the land is wonderful! I can hear water, and goats and sheep. It's just like God said it would be. The land of milk and honey.

Palti: Yeah, it's pretty wonderful, all right.

Igal: So what's the problem? Why can't we come here like God said?

Nahbi: You know those men, and walls, and cities you can't see? Well, they're EVERYWHERE! And they don't look like they'd want to share!

Igal: And what do Caleb and Joshua want to do?

Palti: They want us all—including our wives and our children—to march into this land and claim it as ours!

Igal: But doesn't it belong to us?

Shammua: Yes, but I don't think these people care about that. They'll fight to keep it.

Igal: So Joshua and Caleb are wrong?

Palti: Right.

Igal: (*Confused.*) Joshua and Caleb are right?

Nahbi: No, no. Joshua and Caleb think that God is going to help us.

Igal: And God isn't going to help us?

Shammua: (*Explaining.*) Look. God gave us brains to think with. And any idiot can see that there's no way we can fight off all these people!

Igal: I see. No, I don't see . . . I guess.

Palti: Let's face it, Igal, you can't see anything!

Puppet Production Tips

Kids love puppets! Puppets capture the attention and imagination of children and adults of all ages. Whether you're an experienced puppeteer or a first-timer, there are any number of ways to use puppets in your VBS program. This article has helpful guidelines for successfully using puppets to communicate with students, as well as suggested activities for your puppets.

Gadget Dog Puppet is designed specifically for the SonForce Kids VBS. The puppet is available from Gospel Light, or you can find instructions to make your own in *Reproducible Resources.*

Suggested Activities

Although the Gadget Dog Puppet is used each day in the prekindergarten and kindergarten classes, below are some other ways to use puppets during SonForce Kids VBS.

Welcoming Students Begin each assembly with a puppet welcome. The puppet can also sing a welcome song as students enter assembly room.

Puppet Skits Instead of performing the daily skits with live actors, consider performing the skits with puppets and a stage. The lines can be read live by the puppeteers or recorded ahead of time. You could even play the skit video through your church's sound system (and not display the video) and have the puppets mouth the words and pantomime the action. Be sure to practice the skits ahead of time, and make sure that the audience can easily see the puppets over the stage.

Making Announcements Most people—children AND adults—are notoriously casual listeners. Because puppets are great attention-getters, they provide an effective tool to communicate information that might otherwise be ignored. The format for making announcements might be a conversation between the assembly leader and the puppet. Either the puppet or the adult could be ignorant of the information. The information may need to be repeated several times before the puppet or adult under-stands. By this time, the students will be trying to help give the right information!

An alternate approach would be to have the puppet read the announcement and another puppet interrupt and ask questions.

If the puppeteer is experienced and capable, consider having the puppet pantomime the subject of the announcement, while students try to guess the activity the puppet is acting out.

Giving Directions Students often accept directions faster from a puppet than from an adult. Use a puppet to gain the immediate attention of the group. Then let the puppet give clear, concise directions. For example, at the conclusion of an assembly, a puppet can dismiss each class in turn. The puppet can announce the center each class is to go to or announce a change in the schedule.

Reviewing Bible Verses Use puppets to teach and review Bible verses. Consider these suggestions:

>> Use a puppet to repeat a Bible verse to the students. Students echo the verse.

>> The assembly leader tries to teach a Bible verse to the puppet, but the puppet has trouble learning the verse. Encourage students to help the puppet.

Leader Lines Use the dialog provided for the Assembly Leader to create a conversation between the puppet and the leader. In addition, the puppet could lead the audience in responding to the leader's questions. Or reverse roles and have the puppet ask the questions and the leader lead responses.

Tips for Using Puppets

>> Don't worry about the professional quality of the performance! However, imagination and enthusiasm are essential.

>> Keep it simple! There is no need for stages, props and scenery. The real interest is in the puppet itself and the life you as the puppeteer give it.

>> If the thought of being the voice for a puppet makes you feel uncomfortable, let your puppet move and nod or shake its head vigorously to convey its thoughts. Perhaps your puppet is too shy to speak. Students will be eager to assist this shy puppet in helping you understand what he wants. As you feel increasingly comfortable with the puppet, have it speak a few words, opening the puppet's mouth once for each spoken syllable. Don't worry about creating another voice for the puppet; just use your normal voice. After you have gained some experience, pitch your voice high or low to match the puppet's character.

>> Give your puppet an identifiable personality. Your puppet can be shy, outgoing, happy, sad, regal and dignified, pompous, the country type, a grouch, etc. Or, the puppet can have a few favorite words that it usually says. Students will soon know what to expect when they see the puppet and will look forward to his or her part of the assemblies.

>> Consider having your Youth Helpers perform the puppet skits. This is an effective ministry for middle and high school youth. Not only do they add youthful exuberance to the project, but this is also a ministry they really enjoy.

Making Your Puppet Stage

A puppet stage is not necessary for all puppet work. Dialogue between the Assembly Leader and a puppet is quite effective using Gadget Dog Puppet (available from Gospel Light) or another handheld puppet. However, if you wish to use more than one puppet or to present the daily skits as puppet plays, then a stage is needed.

Below are plans for building a traveling puppet stage. It is large when set up, but easily disassembled. Once disassembled, it is quite compact—easy to move and easy to store. When set up, the stage dimensions are 8 feet (2.4 m) wide and 4 feet (1.2 m) deep. The front panel and sides are 4 feet (1.2 m) tall and the back panel is 6 feet (1.8 m) tall.

Materials Checklist

Note: Use PVC pipe that is 1 inch (2.5 cm) in diameter.

>> 10 8-foot (2.4-m) sections of pipe
>> 3 couplings
>> 2 4-way connectors
>> 6 3-way connectors
>> 2 90-degree elbow fittings
>> 2 tee connectors
>> covering (butcher paper, fabric, etc.)

coupling

3-way connector

4-way connector

90-degree elbow fitting

tee connector

Preparation: Cut each length of PVC pipe into 4-foot (1.2-m) sections. Cut one of the resulting pieces into two 2-foot (.6-m) sections.

Procedure: In a large, flat area, make a large rectangle from six of the 4-foot (1.2-m) PVC sections (sketch a on p. 64). Use a coupling to join the two sections of pipe that make each of the long sides. Place a 4-way connector at each of the top corners, connecting to one of the straight-edge openings. Place a 3-way at the bottom two corners. (Note: For each of the 3-way and 4-way connectors, an opening should be facing up.)

Place one of the 2-foot (.6-m) sections in each of the 4-way connectors, extending the sides of the rectangle (sketch b on p. 64). Connect two 4-foot (1.2-m) sections with a coupling to form the top edge. With a 90-degree elbow fitting at each corner, attach top section to the sides.

Place two 4-foot (1.2-m) sections next to each other on the ground. Connect the two with a tee connector. Make sure the opening is pointed down. At each end, place a 3-way connector. Connect a 4-foot (1.2-m) section to the tee connector and place another tee connector at the bottom. Make sides by placing a 4-foot (1.2-m) section in each of the 3-way connectors. Make the bottom of the rectangle by attaching 4-foot (1.2-m) sections of pipe to 3-way connectors and tee connector (sketch c).

To assemble stage, ask helpers to hold each stage section so that the openings in the 3-way connectors are facing each other. Attach the end of a 4-foot

(1.2-m) section to each 3-way connector (see sketch d). This should give you a large cube, with the back piece taller than the rest (see sketch d).

Tape lengths of butcher paper over the frame to cover it. The butcher paper could be plain or painted with an appropriate scene. Instead of a paper covering, you could use a shower curtain or sew curtains from fabric. If you choose to sew your own, use hook and loop fabric tape to secure the casing at the top of each fabric panel instead of sewing it closed. This will enable you to easily remove the curtains for cleaning or storage.

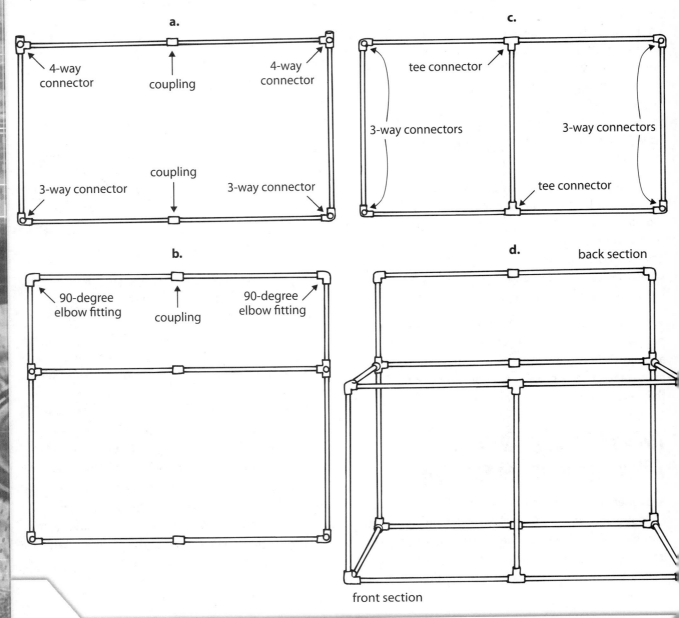

a.
4-way connector
coupling
4-way connector
3-way connector
coupling
3-way connector

b.
90-degree elbow fitting
coupling
90-degree elbow fitting

c.
tee connector
3-way connectors
3-way connectors
tee connector

d. back section

front section